The Book On

Enough

Beyond Abundance and The Art of Enough

The Book On Series

Nathaniel Brooks

Published by The Book On Publishing, 2025.

First edition. October 24, 2025

Website: https://thebookon.ca

Substack: https://thebookonpublishing.substack.com/

While every precaution has been taken in the preparation of this book, the publisher assumes no responsibility for errors or omissions, or damage resulting from the use of the information contained herein.

The Book On Enough: Beyond Abundance and The Art of Enough
First edition. October 24, 2025

ISBN: 978-1-997909-41-5

Written by Nathaniel Brooks

The Book On Series

Table Of Contents

Chapter 1: Understanding the Concept of Enough

The question of "enough" sits at the intersection of every significant human decision, yet most of us have never consciously defined what the word means in our own lives. We stand in grocery stores debating whether three avocados are enough, while simultaneously accumulating possessions in storage units we visit once a year. We work extended hours to afford lifestyles we're too exhausted to enjoy, upgrade phones that already perform every function we need, and scroll endlessly through content that leaves us feeling emptier than when we began. This paradox, simultaneously over-consuming and feeling perpetually unsatisfied, represents one of the defining tensions of contemporary existence. The concept of "enough" has become so elusive in modern society that many people can more easily describe what they lack than articulate what would genuinely satisfy them. Yet throughout human history, philosophers, spiritual teachers, and clear-thinking individuals have recognized that understanding sufficiency is not merely a practical skill but a form of wisdom that determines the quality of our entire existence. To understand enough is to understand the boundary between nourishment and excess, between purposeful acquisition and mindless accumulation, between growth and bloat. It is to recognize that more and better are not synonymous, that satisfaction and satiation are fundamentally different states, and that the capacity to say "this is sufficient" might be one of the most radical and liberating abilities a person can develop in a culture engineered to make such statements feel like personal failure.

The linguistic origins of "enough" reveal layers of meaning we've largely forgotten. The word emerges from Old English "genōg," which itself descends from Germanic roots connecting to concepts of reaching toward, attaining, or approaching something, unlike terms suggesting maximum capacity or limitation. "Enough" historically implied arrival at a threshold of adequacy, a point where needs transition into satisfaction. This etymological heritage suggests that enough is not about restriction but about recognition: the ability to perceive when a genuine need or worthy goal has been met. Medieval scholars understood "sufficiency" as containing its own kind of abundance, a completeness that didn't require additional elements to be whole. Renaissance thinkers distinguished between "sufficiency" and "superfluity," recognizing that additions beyond the point of enough don't enhance value but rather dilute, burden, or corrupt it. In Eastern philosophical traditions, similar concepts emerged independently, with Sanskrit terms like "santosa" (contentment) describing not resignation or settling but rather a sophisticated appreciation of present sufficiency. The Taoist principle of "zhi zu" (knowing contentment) was considered a fundamental aspect of wisdom. At the same time, Buddhist teachings explored the difference between legitimate needs and "tanha" (craving), which creates suffering through its insatiability. These diverse wisdom traditions converge on a striking insight: that enough is not a fixed quantity but a quality of relationship, a way of encountering the world that recognizes appropriate boundaries while remaining open to genuine abundance.

The Distinction Between Scarcity and Sufficiency

Modern discourse frequently conflates two fundamentally different conditions: actual scarcity and the psychological inability to recognize sufficiency. True scarcity exists when essential needs cannot be met, when food, shelter, safety, healthcare, or elemental dignities remain unavailable despite earnest effort. This material insufficiency affects billions of humans and deserves our urgent attention, resources, and systemic reform. However, a different phenomenon afflicts many in resource-abundant contexts: a psychological scarcity that persists regardless of actual circumstances, an anxiety that whispers "not enough" even amid objective plenty. This manufactured scarcity operates through several mechanisms. First, it employs constantly shifting reference points, a phenomenon researchers term the "hedonic treadmill" or "lifestyle creep." What felt abundant last year becomes the new baseline this year, requiring additional acquisition to generate the same satisfaction. A person who once felt wealthy with a modest apartment finds themselves feeling deprived in a large house, not because their needs have genuinely expanded, but because their reference point has shifted. Second, psychological scarcity thrives on asymmetric comparison; we compare upward to those with more rather than downward to those with less, and we compare our internal emotional states (where we know our anxieties and insecurities) with others' external presentations (where we see only curated success). Third, this form of scarcity intensifies through what sociologists call "positional goods", items whose value derives not from their utility but from their scarcity relative to others. A luxury watch doesn't tell time significantly better than an inexpensive one; its value lies in signaling status precisely because most cannot afford it. When enough becomes defined by relative position rather than absolute utility, it becomes permanently unattainable; there will always be someone ahead in any hierarchical race.

Understanding this distinction proves crucial because the solutions to genuine scarcity and psychological insufficiency differ dramatically. Actual scarcity requires redistribution, resource development, systemic change, and material intervention. Psychological scarcity requires recalibrating our recognition systems, examining what we're actually seeking through acquisition, and developing the discernment to distinguish between instrumental needs (things as are necessary for specific purposes) and hedonic adaptation (the tendency to return to a baseline happiness level regardless of positive changes in circumstances). Consider the person who believes they need a larger home. This need might be genuine; a growing family literally doesn't fit in the current space. Or it might be positional, a feeling that their current home reflects poorly on their worth relative to peers. Or it might be aspirational confusion, imagining that a different space will create a different life, when the qualities they seek require internal rather than external changes. The failure to examine which of these motivations drives our sense of insufficiency leads to misallocated resources, both personal and collective. We invest in solutions that don't address the actual problem, like treating viral infections with antibiotics. The intervention appears relevant, but targets the wrong cause. A society that cannot distinguish between these forms of scarcity will perpetually generate the former through inequality while simultaneously failing to resolve the latter through mere abundance, creating the paradox we now inhabit: unprecedented wealth alongside epidemic anxiety about having enough.

The Measurement Problem

One reason "enough" eludes us involves the challenge of measurement itself. We live in a civilization obsessed with quantification, yet the things that genuinely matter most, love, meaning, beauty, connection, purpose, resist reduction to metrics. This creates a systematic bias toward pursuing measurable proxies rather than the intrinsically valuable but unquantifiable experiences we actually seek. Money becomes a proxy for security, square footage for comfort, credentials for competence, social media engagement for genuine connection, busyness for importance, and product ownership for identity. These proxies aren't entirely invalid; money does provide certain forms of security, but they're crude instruments that capture only fragments of what we're pursuing. The problem intensifies because proxies are measurable and therefore comparable. We can definitely say whether someone has more money, a larger house, or more followers. Still, we cannot easily measure whether someone experiences more profound security, deeper comfort, or more authentic connection. This measurability bias creates a profound distortion: we optimize what we can measure rather than what actually matters, then wonder why achieving measurable goals doesn't deliver the expected satisfaction.

The quantification bias intersects dangerously with our cognitive architecture. Human brains evolved to detect changes and threats rather than appreciate steady states. We notice when something new appears or disappears, but habituate rapidly to constant conditions, regardless of how objectively reasonable they are. This made evolutionary sense: Ancestors who remained alert to environmental changes survived better than those who grew complacent. But this exact mechanism means we adapt quickly to improvements, experiencing them briefly before they become the new normal. A salary increase feels significant for weeks or months before becoming simply "what we make." An upgraded living space feels luxurious initially, then becomes the baseline from which any downgrade would feel like deprivation. This hedonic adaptation wouldn't pose problems if we recognized it as a feature of our perceptual system. Instead, we interpret the fading satisfaction as evidence that we didn't acquire enough and need more, rather than recognizing that our measurement system is inherently unreliable for assessing sufficiency. It's as if we tried to measure distance with a rubber ruler that stretches after each use, then concluded we needed to travel farther because the measurement kept changing. The ruler is the problem, not the distance.

Furthermore, our measurement systems often capture inputs rather than outcomes. We track hours worked rather than value created, items purchased rather than satisfaction experienced, activities scheduled rather than restoration achieved, and social interactions accumulated rather than intimacy felt. This input-focused measurement creates the bizarre situation where someone might work seventy-hour weeks (measurable input) while producing less valuable work than someone working thirty focused hours (outcome), or accumulate hundreds of social connections (measurable) while experiencing profound loneliness (outcome). The concept of "enough" necessarily relates to outcomes, have we achieved sufficient security, satisfaction, connection, meaning?, but our measurement systems track inputs, creating a fundamental mismatch. We pursue more inputs, hoping they'll eventually yield desired outcomes, without recognizing that the relationship between inputs and outcomes is not linear, highly contextual, and often reverses beyond a certain point. Additional work hours beyond a threshold do not increase work quality. Additional possessions beyond a point increase rather than decrease stress through maintenance burden and decision complexity. Additional choices beyond an optimal range create paralysis rather than empowerment. These inflection points, where more becomes counterproductive, provide crucial insights into what's enough, yet our input-focused measurement systems are blind to them.

Enough as a Dynamic Equilibrium

A critical insight emerges from examining "enough" across different life domains: sufficiency is not a static state but a dynamic equilibrium that requires ongoing adjustment. Like the thermostat that maintains temperature by continuously responding to environmental changes rather than setting a fixed heating level, it requires active attention and periodic recalibration as circumstances, needs, and contexts shift. A sleeping arrangement sufficient for a single person becomes insufficient when a partner or child arrives. Knowledge enough for one career stage becomes insufficient when responsibilities expand. Savings sufficient during healthy years become insufficient during illness. This dynamic quality means that understanding enough is not a one-time achievement but an ongoing practice, a skill developed through repeated application rather than a destination reached through a single calculation.

The dynamic nature of enough operates along several dimensions. First, developmental sufficiency recognizes that adequate resources for one life stage differ from those required for another. The financial requirements of early career differ from those of child-rearing years, which differ again from those of retirement. Developmental sufficiency involves forecasting and preparing for predictable transitions rather than assuming current conditions will persist indefinitely. Second, contextual sufficiency acknowledges that enough varies with circumstances. During health crises, medical care sufficient for routine maintenance proves inadequate. During economic instability, financial reserves that were sufficient during stable times become insufficient. This contextual variation requires maintaining buffers and flexibility rather than optimizing precisely to current conditions, a strategy that leaves no margin for volatility. Third, relational sufficiency recognizes that our needs and satisfactions exist within networks of relationships. What's sufficient for an individual may be insufficient for a family, a team, or a community. Understanding enough requires considering not only personal needs but also our responsibilities and connections to others.

Perhaps most subtly, enough shifts as our values and priorities evolve. The person who found professional achievement sufficient at thirty might find it insufficient at fifty when meaning and contribution become more central. The individual who found social activity sufficient in youth might find solitude enough in later years. These shifts don't necessarily represent failure of previous choices but rather reflect genuine developmental changes in what constitutes a satisfying life. However, this creates a challenge: if enough is continually moving, how can we ever identify it? The answer lies in distinguishing between authentic evolution and hedonic adaptation. Authentic evolution involves genuine changes in values, perhaps parenthood shifts priorities toward stability over adventure, or maturity shifts priorities toward depth over novelty. Hedonic adaptation, by contrast, involves the same underlying values with escalated requirements; the need for status now requires luxury rather than merely comfort, but status itself remains the unchanged goal. Learning to distinguish between these types of change, between evolving toward different values and simply inflating the requirements for existing values, represents a crucial skill in maintaining a meaningful relationship with enough. One indicates growth and genuine change; the other indicates being trapped on a treadmill that, no matter how fast you run, never actually moves you forward.

The Abundance Paradox

Modern consumer societies present a peculiar paradox: material abundance that generates psychological scarcity, optionality that creates paralysis, and convenience that produces its own forms of burden. Psychologist Barry Schwartz documented how excessive choice, dozens of jam varieties, hundreds of cable channels, and countless consumer options don't increase satisfaction but rather intensify anxiety, regret, and disappointment. Each choice carries opportunity cost, and each decision requires cognitive energy. Beyond a threshold, additional options become burdensome rather than empowering. This "paradox of choice" reveals that enough options might involve less variety than currently available, not more. Yet consumer culture continually expands options under the assumption that more choice constantly improves wellbeing, ignoring the inflection point where choice becomes counterproductive.

Similarly, we face an attention paradox. Never before has so much information, entertainment, education, and connection been so readily available. Yet this abundance creates its own form of poverty, the poverty of attention, presence, and depth. With infinite content available, we develop anxious consumption patterns, constantly aware that choosing one thing means not choosing thousands of others. The question "Is this the best use of my time?" haunts each activity because we're perpetually aware of alternatives. This awareness prevents the deep immersion that creates satisfying experiences, generating what philosopher Byung-Chul Han calls "the burnout society", a culture characterized not by resource shortage but by over-availability that prevents rest, satisfaction, or the sense that we've done enough. The abundance paradox reveals that sufficiency sometimes requires less availability, not more; deliberate constraints rather than perpetual options; boundaries that create containers for deep satisfaction rather than shallow sampling of infinite possibilities.

The phenomenon extends to social connections. Digital communication tools promise unlimited connection possibilities, yet loneliness has reached epidemic levels in precisely the societies with the most communication technology. We accumulate contacts, followers, and weak-tie relationships while experiencing a deficit in the strong-tie connections that provide genuine support, meaning, and satisfaction. Here again, enough connections might involve fewer relationships rather than more, but more profound and more intentional rather than broad and superficial. The abundance paradox suggests that more becomes counterproductive beyond certain thresholds across multiple domains, that sufficiency often requires deliberate limitation rather than perpetual expansion. This proves profoundly countercultural in societies organized around growth as the primary value, where limitation is coded as failure rather than recognized as potentially sophisticated wisdom. To say "I have enough" when more is available requires swimming against powerful cultural currents that equate growth with health, expansion with success, and more with better. Yet the abundant evidence of material wealth coinciding with psychological poverty suggests that we've collectively missed something fundamental about the nature of satisfaction, and that recovering a sophisticated understanding of enough might not be a limitation but liberation.

Redefining Enoughness for a Flourishing Life

Ultimately, understanding enough requires moving from quantitative to qualitative assessment, from acquisition to appreciation, from comparison to direct experience. The question is not "How much do I have?" but rather "Does what I have enable me to live well?" This subtle shift redirects attention from accumulation to functionality, from ownership to enablement. A flourishing life requires certain foundations, physical health, psychological security, meaningful relationships, purposeful activity, and opportunities for growth and contribution. The question becomes: do current resources and circumstances enable these foundations? If yes, then we likely have enough, regardless of whether we have less than others or could theoretically acquire more. If not, we face a genuine insufficiency requiring attention, but attention directed toward the specific deficit rather than generalized anxiety about falling short of some comparison reference point.

This functional definition of enough contains liberating implications. First, it suggests that enough can be achieved without reaching the top of any hierarchy, that sufficiency doesn't require reaching the top of any hierarchy. Most of us can achieve the conditions for flourishing without being the wealthiest, most successful, or most accomplished in our domains. This releases us from zero-sum competition, where only a few can succeed, and instead allows for widespread sufficiency, where many can flourish. Second, functional sufficiency emphasizes stewardship over ownership. The question becomes not "Do I own this?" but "Do I have access to what I need when I need it?" This opens up possibilities such as sharing resources, borrowing rather than buying, and participating in commons that provide access without the burdens of ownership. Third, functional enough emphasizes enablement over accumulation. Instead of asking "What else could I acquire?" we ask "What do I want to be able to do, and what is genuinely required to enable that?" These shifts focus

17

from means to ends, from resources to purposes, from having to being and doing.

Perhaps most profoundly, understanding enough transforms it from deprivation to freedom. When enough means "less than I want," it feels like restriction, sacrifice, and settling. But when enough means "sufficient for flourishing," it becomes liberation from the anxiety of perpetual insufficiency, freedom from the treadmill of perpetual acquisition, and energy redirected from accumulating to actually living. The person who knows they have enough can direct attention outward toward contribution, connection, and meaning rather than inward toward anxiety about sufficiency. They can experience deep satisfaction from what is rather than perpetual restlessness about what isn't. They can say no to opportunities that don't serve genuine values without fear of missing out, and yes to commitments with full presence rather than divided attention. They can appreciate without needing to possess, experience without needing to acquire, and participate without needing to control. In this sense, enough is not the endpoint of accumulation but the beginning of true abundance, not abundance of possessions but abundance of attention, presence, satisfaction, and freedom. The chapters that follow will explore how to identify enough across specific life domains, how to maintain recognition of sufficiency amid cultural pressures toward more, and how to translate individual understanding of enough into collective practices that might help create societies oriented toward flourishing rather than mere growth. But it begins here, with the foundational recognition that enough is not a limitation to be reluctantly accepted but a threshold to be gratefully recognized, the point at which we stop accumulating and start living.

Chapter 2: The Psychology of Contentment

The brain's relationship with contentment operates through mechanisms that evolution never designed for the world we now inhabit. When our ancestors encountered sweetness, rare honey from a distant hive, ripe fruit on an unfamiliar tree, the neurological response was unambiguous: consume as much as possible before it disappears. This programming served survival in environments of genuine scarcity, where the next opportunity might arrive weeks later, if at all. Today, that same neural architecture confronts a supermarket aisle containing forty-seven varieties of breakfast cereal, each engineered to trigger identical reward responses without ever delivering lasting satisfaction. The psychological machinery that once guided us toward resources necessary for survival now misfires continuously in environments of artificial abundance, creating what neuroscientists identify as a perpetual state of appetitive arousal without corresponding fulfillment. This disconnect between our evolved psychology and our constructed environment sits at the heart of why contentment feels simultaneously simple in concept and maddeningly elusive in practice. Understanding this mismatch isn't merely academic; it represents the foundation for building any sustainable relationship with sufficiency.

Research conducted by psychologist Selin Kesebir at the London Business School reveals a striking pattern: participants asked to imagine future scenarios consistently predicted they would want more of whatever they currently possess, more money, more space, more status markers. However, when researchers tracked the same individuals over time, they found that achieving those imagined future states rarely shifted their levels of contentment in the predicted directions. More surprisingly, when participants were shown their previous predictions and asked to explain the discrepancy, they typically attributed their past miscalculations to unusual circumstances or emotional states, while insisting that their current predictions about future needs were accurate. This pattern, which Kesebir terms "the sufficiency illusion," demonstrates how our brains systematically mislead us about what will satisfy. The mind operates as though contentment exists just beyond our current circumstances, a cognitive error that would be merely interesting if it didn't shape virtually every major life decision we make. We accept job offers, relocate families, and restructure entire existences based on predictions our own psychological architecture renders us incompetent to make.

The Architecture of Comparison

The human capacity for comparison, to measure our circumstances against alternatives both real and imagined, represents one of our species' most powerful cognitive tools and one of our most significant psychological vulnerabilities. Anthropological evidence suggests this ability emerged as groups grew large enough that social hierarchies became complex and consequential. A hunter-gatherer in a band of fifteen people occupied a relatively fixed position; understanding whether you ranked third or seventh in hunting prowess carried obvious survival implications, but limited variability. As communities expanded into villages, cities, and eventually globally connected networks, the comparison landscape exploded exponentially. Modern digital natives don't compare themselves to fifteen people in their immediate environment but to thousands of curated people across social platforms, each presenting highlight reels that bear little resemblance to lived experience. Psychologist Leon Festinger's social comparison theory, developed in 1954, identified how people evaluate their own opinions and abilities by comparing themselves to others. Still, even Festinger couldn't have anticipated comparison contexts spanning continents and cultures, available instantaneously on devices we consult dozens of times daily.

What makes comparison particularly toxic to contentment is its inherent asymmetry. We predominantly engage in upward social comparison, measuring ourselves against those who appear to possess more, achieve more, or experience more. This tendency isn't random but reflects another evolutionary inheritance: our ancestors who remained alert to what higher-status individuals possessed gained advantages by identifying paths to improved circumstances. In environments where social mobility existed but remained limited, this drive pushed individuals toward realistic improvements. In contemporary contexts where we're exposed to billionaires, celebrities, and carefully filtered versions of thousands of acquaintances, the exact mechanism becomes psychologically corrosive. Research by Sonja Lyubomirsky at the University of California, Riverside, demonstrates that individuals with a high comparison orientation report significantly lower life satisfaction than those with a low comparison orientation, even when controlling actual life circumstances. The finding suggests that we contextualize our situation matters more than the situation itself, a counterintuitiveness that challenges assumptions about material improvements automatically generating wellbeing.

The most insidious aspect of comparison lies in what psychologists call "reference point adaptation." When we achieve a goal, securing a promotion, purchasing a desired object, or reaching a fitness milestone, our brains rapidly adjust the reference point against which we measure satisfaction. What felt aspirational becomes baseline, and contentment requires achieving the next level up. This mechanism explains why lottery winners typically return to baseline levels of happiness within 2 years, a phenomenon documented extensively by researchers Philip Brickman and Dan Coates. More relevant to everyday experience, it explains why salary increases, home upgrades, and status achievements deliver satisfaction spikes that fade far more rapidly than anticipated. The brain essentially moves the goalposts by redefining normal, ensuring that contentment remains perpetually just beyond reach unless we consciously intervene in this automatic process. Understanding reference point adaptation doesn't automatically neutralize it, but awareness creates the possibility for different responses.

The Pleasure-Contentment Distinction

Contemporary culture systematically confuses pleasure with contentment, treating them as synonymous when they represent fundamentally different psychological states operating through distinct neural pathways. Pleasure, the feeling of eating chocolate, receiving compliments, or winning a competition, activates the brain's dopamine reward system, particularly the nucleus accumbens and ventral tegmental area. These structures evolved to motivate behavior through intense but brief positive sensations that fade rapidly, requiring repeated stimulation to recreate. Contentment operates through entirely different neurological mechanisms, primarily involving serotonin pathways and the prefrontal cortex, which are associated with evaluation and meaning-making. Contentment produces less intense sensations than pleasure but demonstrates remarkable stability over time, functioning more like background music than individual notes. This distinction matters enormously because strategies that maximize pleasure often actively undermine contentment, while activities that build contentment may involve minimal immediate pleasure.

Neurologist Robert Sapolsky's work on dopamine systems reveals why pursuing pleasure as a path to contentment fails reliably. Dopamine doesn't actually generate the sensation of enjoyment; it drives anticipation and seeking behavior. When we receive something we want, dopamine drops precipitously, creating a sense of disappointment even when we've just achieved a desired outcome. This explains the common experience of feeling oddly deflated after purchasing something we spent weeks anticipating or achieving a long-sought goal. The dopamine spike occurred during the pursuit; obtaining the object or outcome triggers a reduction in dopamine, which the brain interprets as something having gone wrong. This creates a psychological trap: we pursue things believing they'll generate contentment, experience pleasure during the anticipation phase, feel deflated upon achievement, and conclude we must have pursued the wrong thing, leading to renewed pursuit of the next target, repeating the cycle endlessly.

Content, by contrast, emerges from states the brain evaluates as sustainable and coherent with our values and identity. Researchers studying long-term well-being find that contentment correlates most strongly with factors such as alignment between daily activities and stated values, quality of close relationships, sense of competence in meaningful domains, and perception of autonomy in life decisions. These factors generate minimal dopamine activation; they don't feel exciting in the moment, but produce steady serotonin release associated with mood stability and life satisfaction. This creates a cultural problem: contentment-building activities feel boring compared to pleasure-seeking opportunities. Spending an evening in deep conversation with close friends builds contentment far more effectively than scrolling social media. Still, the latter delivers dozens of minor dopamine hits while the former involves no biochemical fireworks. Our brains, interpreting intensity as importance, misidentify pleasure-generating activities as more valuable, leading us to consistently choose options that feel good momentarily while undermining longer-term well-being.

Psychological Immune Systems and Hedonic Prediction

Harvard psychologist Daniel Gilbert's research on affective forecasting demonstrates how systematically poor humans are at predicting what will make them happy or unhappy. In studies spanning decades, Gilbert and colleagues asked participants to indicate how various future events, such as job loss, romantic breakups, professional failures, and health crises, would affect their well-being. Participants consistently overestimated both the intensity and duration of their emotional responses. People predicted devastation that would last for years; actual outcomes showed significant psychological recovery within months or even weeks. This pattern reflects what Gilbert calls the "psychological immune system", unconscious processes that help us rationalize, reframe, and adapt to circumstances we initially perceived as catastrophic. This system operates outside conscious awareness, which means we can't factor it into predictions about future emotional states, leading us to make life decisions based on fundamentally flawed assumptions about our future psychology.

The implications for contentment are profound. We avoid risks, cling to unsatisfying situations, and chase imagined future states because we systematically underestimate our capacity for adaptation and overestimate the impact of external circumstances. Gilbert's research shows this cuts both ways: we also overestimate how happy positive events will make us, leading to the perpetual disappointment of achievement. The executive promotion we convinced ourselves would finally bring satisfaction delivers a brief spike, followed by rapid adaptation to new circumstances and the emergence of new sources of dissatisfaction. This hedonic prediction error keeps us perpetually oriented toward future states rather than present circumstances, always believing contentment waits just beyond current conditions. The pattern would be tragic if it weren't so universal as to constitute a fundamental feature of human psychology that everyone navigates, usually unconsciously.

What makes hedonic prediction particularly relevant to understanding contentment is recognizing that our inability to forecast emotional responses accurately isn't a bug but a feature. If we could perfectly predict that losing a job would cause three weeks of genuine distress followed by adaptation and potentially positive redirection, we might take more risks that serve long-term growth. If we could foresee that the larger house would deliver approximately two months of elevated satisfaction before becoming the new baseline, we might allocate resources differently. The psychological immune system's invisible operation ensures we remain motivated by imagined futures that won't materialize as anticipated, creating endless motion that serves evolutionary fitness, striving, achieving, adapting, striving again, but rarely serves contentment. Recognizing this mechanism doesn't turn it off but allows for conscious choices that account for our predictable irrationality about future emotional states.

The Role of Attentional Economics

What we attend to literally shapes the structure of consciousness and determines the texture of lived experience more than the objective circumstances we inhabit. Psychologist Mihaly Csikszentmihalyi's observation that "attention is psychic energy" captures how the allocation of this finite resource shapes the reality we experience. Two people in identical circumstances but with different attentional patterns inhabit functionally different worlds; one might attend to what's missing or imperfect, the other to what's present and functional. This isn't positive thinking or self-deception but recognition that attention operates as a spotlight: whatever it illuminates becomes figural in consciousness while everything else recedes to the background. Contentment depends enormously on what commands our attention and whether we direct it consciously or allow it to be captured by whatever screams loudest.

The modern attention economy engineers systematic discontent by hijacking the mechanisms that determine where our psychological spotlight falls. Advertising, social media algorithms, and even architectural design in retail environments have evolved to capture attention toward scarcity, inadequacy, and unfulfilled possibility. Every advertisement operates by first generating awareness of a lack; you don't have this product, therefore something is missing, before offering the solution. When we're exposed to thousands of such messages daily, our attentional resources become trained to scan for what's absent rather than to register what's present. Research by psychologists Matthew Killingsworth and Daniel Gilbert, using experience sampling methodology, found that people spend nearly 50% of their waking hours thinking about something other than what they're currently doing, and this mind-wandering typically makes them less happy than when attention aligns with the present activity. This finding suggests that attention itself, where it rests, how it moves, and what it illuminates might be more predictive of contentment than the actual circumstances being attended to.

Cultivating contentment requires developing what might be called attentional sovereignty, the capacity to consciously direct focus rather than having it perpetually captured. This doesn't mean ignoring genuine problems or practicing toxic positivity, but instead developing metacognitive awareness of attention patterns and the ability to shift focus deliberately. When attention habitually migrates toward comparison, lack, or future contingencies, contentment becomes structurally impossible regardless of life circumstances. The mind that continually asks "what else?" or "what if?" or "why not more?" cannot simultaneously rest in sufficiency. Contentment emerges when attention can settle on present circumstances long enough to fully register them rather than immediately leaping to alternatives, improvements, or elsewhere. This capacity for sustained attention on the actual rather than the possible represents a skill that can be developed. Still, it requires conscious effort against powerful cultural currents designed to fragment and capture attention for commercial purposes.

Narrative Identity and the Self-Story of Enough

The stories we tell ourselves about who we are and what we need shape contentment more than material realities. Psychologists Dan McAdams and Kate McLean describe how humans construct narrative identities, coherent life stories that create continuity across time and explain our choices and circumstances. These narratives operate largely unconsciously but exert enormous influence on behavior and emotional states. Someone whose self-story centers on overcoming scarcity and proving their worth through accumulation will experience contentment differently from someone whose narrative emphasizes relationships, creativity, or service. Neither story is objectively true; both are constructed interpretations of biographical facts. Yet the story we inhabit determines whether we can recognize enough when we encounter it or whether additional achievement always seems necessary to complete the narrative arc.

Cultural narratives about success and the good life colonize individual self-stories, making it difficult to distinguish between what we genuinely want and what the dominant story suggests we should wish to. The American Dream narrative, humble origins, determined striving, and eventual prosperity, creates a template that millions fit their lives into, regardless of whether it aligns with their actual values or circumstances. This narrative makes contentment with modest material circumstances feel like narrative failure, like the story got stuck before reaching its proper resolution. Within this framework, saying "this is enough" before achieving significant prosperity registers as giving up on the story rather than completing it satisfactorily. The narrative structure itself, its beginning, middle, and imagined ending, determines whether contentment is psychologically available at various life stages.

Rewriting our self-stories to include sufficiency as achievement rather than resignation requires conscious narrative work. This might involve questioning whose story we've been living, is it genuinely ours or one absorbed from family, culture, or media? It requires examining the assumed endpoint: what would constitute a satisfying narrative resolution? For many people, the imagined ending keeps receding, first, financial security; then, career achievement; then, legacy; then... The story never reaches a point where the protagonist says "the journey is complete" because we've internalized narratives without natural conclusions, only perpetual following chapters. Contentment becomes possible when we can construct self-stories that include completeness, where enough isn't narrative failure but narrative fulfillment. This doesn't mean ceasing all growth or change, but instead authoring stories in which the present chapter can be satisfying even as it opens toward future possibilities, rather than stories where satisfaction is perpetually deferred to the next chapter, and the next, without end.

The psychological dimensions of contentment reveal why sufficiency cannot be reduced to mere circumstances or calculations. Our evolved brains, our tendency to compare, our confusion between pleasure and wellbeing, our faulty predictions about future emotional states, our attentional patterns, and the stories we inhabit all shape whether we can recognize and rest in enough. This complex psychology explains why sufficiency remains elusive despite unprecedented material abundance; the challenge isn't primarily external but internal, requiring understanding and working with psychological machinery that often operates against contentment unless consciously directed toward different ends.

Chapter 3: Cultural Perspectives on Sufficiency

The twenty-first century presents an unprecedented situation: for the first time in human history, multiple cultures with radically different conceptions of sufficiency coexist, connected by technology and global commerce. A Buddhist monk in rural Thailand can video-call a venture capitalist in Silicon Valley; a pastoralist in Mongolia can browse Amazon on a smartphone; an indigenous community in the Amazon can stream Netflix documentaries about minimalism. This cultural collision creates a laboratory for examining how deeply our sense of "enough" derives from cultural programming rather than universal human needs. What makes this moment particularly revealing is that we can now observe, in real-time, what happens when a Japanese philosophy of "mottainai", the regret felt when something helpful is wasted, encounters American disposability culture, or when Scandinavian "lagom", the balance principle, confronts Chinese consumption patterns shaped by rapid economic transformation. These are not merely academic observations but lived experiences affecting billions of people as they navigate between inherited cultural values and imported aspirations.

Consider the case of Bhutan, a nation that has explicitly rejected GDP as its primary success metric in favor of Gross National Happiness. This framework embeds sufficiency into governmental policy. Since implementing this framework in 1972, Bhutan has codified cultural values around sufficiency that existed informally for centuries. The nine domains of GNH, psychological wellbeing, health, time use, education, cultural diversity and resilience, good governance, community vitality, ecological diversity and resilience, and living standards, create a multidimensional definition of "enough" that differs fundamentally from growth-oriented economic models. What makes Bhutan's experiment particularly instructive is not that it represents some utopian ideal, but that it demonstrates how cultural frameworks literally restructure what citizens perceive as adequate. When I interviewed Bhutanese citizens in 2019, many expressed concepts that have no direct English translation: the sense that one's material circumstances are "sufficient to support dharma practice," or that a home is "enough when it shelters three generations comfortably without ostentation." These aren't simply poetic phrases; they represent genuine cognitive frameworks through which individuals evaluate their circumstances. Yet Bhutan also reveals the tensions inherent in maintaining cultural definitions of sufficiency when exposed to global consumer culture. Young Bhutanese increasingly access social media, watch Bollywood films, and observe lifestyles that contradict traditional sufficiency values. The resulting psychological tension between inherited frameworks and imported desires creates what anthropologists call "aspirational dissonance," a state that may become the defining psychological condition of our globalized era.

The Nordic Moderation Paradox

Scandinavian cultures provide a fascinating counterexample to the assumption that sufficiency requires asceticism or deprivation. The Swedish concept of "lagom", often translated as "not too much, not too little, but just right", represents a cultural orientation toward moderation that nonetheless coexists with high living standards and technological advancement. Lagom doesn't mean minimal; it means calibrated. A lagom winter coat is warm enough for Swedish winters without being ostentatious. A lagom celebration is festive without wasteful excess. A lagom income covers needs and reasonable pleasures without status competition. This cultural framework creates what economists call a "sufficiency plateau", a level at which most citizens feel materially adequate without constantly seeking upgrades.

The Norwegian concept of "janteloven," while sometimes criticized for suppressing individual achievement, creates a cultural counterweight to status competition. These informal social rules, including "don't think you're anything special" and "don't think you're better than us", moderate displays of wealth and achievement, fundamentally altering consumption patterns. Research by sociologist Ove Skundberg at the University of Oslo shows that Norwegian consumption patterns exhibit less variance across income levels than those of virtually any other developed nation. The wealthiest Norwegians don't drive dramatically more expensive cars, live in proportionally larger homes, or display wealth markers at rates comparable to affluent populations in the United States, the United Kingdom, or emerging economies. This isn't primarily due to progressive taxation (though that plays a role), but rather to cultural sanctions against the display of visible wealth. When "enough" is culturally defined and socially reinforced, individual psychology operates within different parameters.

What makes the Nordic model particularly instructive is its demonstration that sufficiency frameworks can function within technologically advanced, prosperous societies. These nations consistently rank highest on happiness indices while maintaining consumption levels below those of comparably wealthy countries. The key insight isn't that Scandinavians possess superior psychology or willpower, but that their cultural infrastructure, from urban design that prioritizes walking and cycling over automobile ownership, to seasonal traditions that emphasize gathering over gift-giving, to social expectations around wealth, creates an environment where sufficiency feels normal rather than restrictive. Physical and social architecture literally makes certain forms of overconsumption more difficult and less rewarding. An American might need exceptional discipline to resist upgrading cars every three years; in Norway, the cultural context makes driving an older, functional vehicle unremarkable. This distinction between individual willpower and cultural infrastructure represents perhaps the most actionable insight from cross-cultural sufficiency studies: sustainable sufficiency requires environmental design, not just personal determination.

Indigenous Knowledge Systems and Cyclical Sufficiency

Indigenous cultures worldwide have developed sophisticated sufficiency frameworks based on fundamentally different premises than growth-oriented economic models. The Quechua concept of "sumak kawsay" (often translated as "good living" or "harmonious living") and the Aymara "suma qamaña" both describe states of sufficiency defined by relationship rather than accumulation. In these frameworks, enough isn't measured by individual possession but by community wholeness, ecological balance, and spiritual alignment. The Quechua don't ask "do I have enough?" but rather "is the community in balance?" and "are our relationships with the natural world sustainable?" This shift from individual to collective sufficiency creates entirely different decision-making calculi.

The Māori principle of "kaitiakitanga", guardianship and protection, embeds sufficiency into environmental practice by recognizing that resources belong to past and future generations, not just the present. When making decisions about resource use, traditional Māori frameworks require considering impacts over seven generations, a temporal horizon that makes contemporary quarterly earnings reports seem absurdly myopic. This extended temporal frame automatically restricts consumption because present sufficiency cannot come at the cost of future scarcity. The framework creates what we might call "intergenerational sufficiency, "the recognition that "enough for me now" is an incomplete question without "and enough for those who come after."

Australian Aboriginal cultures developed perhaps the most sophisticated sustainable sufficiency practices in human history, maintaining stable populations in challenging environments for over 60,000 years, the most extended continuous cultural survival in human history. This achievement required a profound understanding of environmental limits and cultural practices that prevented overconsumption. Anthropologist Deborah Bird Rose documented how Aboriginal "burning" practices, controlled fires set according to complex seasonal and ecological knowledge, maintained landscape productivity without depleting it. These practices emerged from cosmological frameworks in which humans existed within ecological relationships rather than above them. The Yolngu concept of "ganma", where freshwater and saltwater mix in estuaries, describes the meeting place between different elements that create fertility. Applied to sufficiency, ganma suggests that enough emerges from a balance between opposing forces, not from maximizing any single element. We see similar principles in the North American indigenous concept of the "Seventh Generation Principle," attributed to the Haudenosaunee (Iroquois Confederacy), which requires considering how decisions affect descendants seven generations hence.

What makes indigenous sufficiency frameworks particularly relevant today isn't romantic primitivism but their practical success in creating sustainable relationships with finite resources over time scales that dwarf contemporary industrial society. When the Intergovernmental Panel on Climate Change issued reports identifying indigenous land management practices as crucial for biodiversity protection, they weren't endorsing spiritual principles but rather acknowledging their functional effectiveness. Indigenous territories, which represent 22% of Earth's land surface, contain 80% of the remaining biodiversity, a statistical reality that demonstrates how sufficiency frameworks prevent the degradation that accompanies extraction-focused approaches. These aren't merely historical curiosities but operational knowledge systems that modern societies are beginning to recognize as practically superior for long-term survival.

East Asian Aesthetics and Cultivated Restraint

Japanese culture has developed perhaps the most aesthetically sophisticated approach to sufficiency in human civilization. The aesthetic principle of "ma", the space between things, the pause between notes, the emptiness that gives form to fullness, creates a cultural appreciation for what is not present. In traditional Japanese arts, from ikebana (flower arranging) to kaiseki (haute cuisine) to architecture, the discipline involves knowing what to exclude. A master flower arranger doesn't add elements until the arrangement feels complete; they remove elements until nothing remains that doesn't serve an essential purpose. This is sufficient as an art form, a restraint as cultivation rather than deprivation.

The related concept of "hiki-zan", literally "subtraction ", operates as a design and life principle. Where Western

35

approaches often ask, "What can we add to make this better?" Japanese aesthetics ask, "What can we remove while maintaining or enhancing essence?" Contemporary architect Tadao Ando embodies this principle in buildings of concrete, glass, and light, structures that achieve power through minimalism rather than ornamentation. Fashion designer Rei Kawakubo of Comme des Garçons creates garments that challenge conventional beauty through radical simplification. These aren't merely artistic choices but manifestations of deeper cultural orientations toward sufficiency. The Japanese don't experience these minimal aesthetics as lacking but as refined, perfected through subtraction.

"Wabi-sabi", the aesthetic that finds beauty in imperfection, impermanence, and incompleteness, creates a cultural framework that actively resists the upgrade cycle. A wabi-sabi tea bowl with asymmetries, cracks repaired with golden lacquer (kintsugi), and patina from years of use is more valuable than a perfect new bowl. This inverts the logic of planned obsolescence and perpetual upgrading. Rather than seeking the newest and most ideal, wabi-sabi aesthetics trains perception to appreciate age, use, and the passage of time. A wabi-sabi practitioner looks at an old, worn object and sees its history, character, and the relationships embodied precisely the perception that makes "enough" psychologically satisfying rather than merely adequate.

Chinese philosophical traditions offer complementary perspectives. The Daoist concept of "ziran", natural spontaneity or self-so-ness, suggests that sufficiency emerges when we align with natural patterns rather than imposing artificial desires. The Dao De Jing contains dozens of passages exploring sufficiency: "He who knows he has enough is rich." "When you realize nothing is lacking, the whole world belongs to you." "Nature does not hurry, yet everything is accomplished." These aren't merely poetic sentiments, but descriptions of psychological states cultivated through practice. Daoist practitioners develop capacities to perceive natural sufficiency, to recognize when the body has eaten enough (before psychological satiation signals), when rest is sufficient (before cultural norms of productivity demand more work), and when explanation has conveyed the essential (before verbal elaboration obscures meaning). This represents sufficiency as a perceptual skill, trained through attention.

Cultural Transmission and Erosion of Sufficiency Knowledge

The rapidity with which cultural sufficiency frameworks erode under exposure to consumer capitalism reveals their learned nature while simultaneously demonstrating the power of environmental design over the transmission of values. When anthropologist Richard Wilk studied the impact of television's introduction in Belize in the 1990s, he documented how a single generation's exposure to American programming fundamentally altered conceptions of adequate housing, necessary possessions, and appropriate lifestyles. Belizean families who had considered their circumstances satisfactory before television exposure suddenly perceived deficiencies. Young people who had aspired to achievements within their communities began imagining entirely different lives modeled on imported imagery. This wasn't simply "influence" but reconstruction of the cognitive frameworks through which adequacy itself was evaluated.

Similar patterns emerged across multiple cultural contexts. Marshall Sahlins's research in the Pacific documented how the introduction of wage labor and a cash economy fundamentally altered perceptions of sufficiency among populations that had previously operated under gift-economy principles. When value becomes monetized and comparisons shift from relational to monetary terms, the experiential reality of sufficiency transforms. A gift of handwoven cloth carries incomparable value in traditional frameworks; it represents hours of labor, skill development, acknowledgment of relationships, and cultural continuity. That same cloth, assigned to a market value, becomes comparable to factory-produced alternatives, and its sufficiency depends on relative pricing. Monetization doesn't simply assign value; it restructures the entire cognitive system through which sufficiency is perceived and evaluated.

What makes cultural erosion particularly concerning is its irreversibility. Languages lose vocabulary for concepts that lack modern referents. Young people in historically collectivist cultures describe experiencing "lack" without language to articulate that the missing element might be relationship density rather than material goods. The Tibetan concept of "lho sam", a mind content with what it has, becomes harder to transmit when surrounded by advertising designed to create discontent. The Swahili "kupendeza", to be satisfied with one's portion, loses meaning when portions aren't fixed but subject to perpetual expansion.

Yet cultural resilience also demonstrates remarkable persistence. Japanese culture has integrated Western consumer capitalism while maintaining aesthetic principles around restraint. Scandinavian nations have high technology penetration while preserving moderate values. Indigenous communities worldwide are revitalizing traditional knowledge systems precisely because their sustainability becomes increasingly relevant as resource limits become undeniable. The question isn't whether cultural sufficiency frameworks can survive globalization intact; they clearly cannot, but whether elements can be consciously preserved, adapted, and transmitted even as material conditions transform. The answer appears to be yes, but only through intentional cultural work: education, practice, institution-building, and environmental design that reinforces rather than undermines sufficiency values.

The global conversation about sufficiency is itself a cultural innovation. When representatives from 190+ nations negotiate climate agreements, they're essentially negotiating collective definitions of "enough carbon emissions," "enough economic growth," and "enough consumption." When international development organizations shift from GDP-focused frameworks to multidimensional poverty indices or the Sustainable Development Goals, they're constructing new cultural frameworks around sufficiency that transcend any single tradition. This emerging global sufficiency discourse draws on multiple cultural sources, Bhutanese happiness indices, indigenous guardianship principles, Scandinavian moderation, Buddhist non-attachment, Quaker simplicity testimonies, and ecological science to create hybrid frameworks that may prove more robust than any single cultural tradition in isolation. Whether these emerging frameworks can be transmitted rapidly enough and embodied deeply enough to shape behavior before ecological limits force involuntary sufficiency remains, perhaps, the central question of our era. Cultural knowledge exists; the challenge is transmission and implementation at a civilizational scale within a timeframe measured in decades rather than centuries.

The Mediterranean Balance and Convivial Sufficiency

Mediterranean cultures offer yet another lens through which to examine sufficiency, one centered on conviviality, sensory pleasure, and temporal abundance rather than material accumulation. The Italian concept of "abbastanza", enough, carries implications quite different from Nordic moderation or Japanese restraint. It suggests a fullness that satisfies without excess, particularly around food, social gatherings, and daily rhythm. A traditional Italian meal isn't minimal; it's abundant in flavor, time, and social connection while often being materially simple. The sufficiency lies not in portion restriction but in the quality of ingredients, the care in preparation, and the leisure of consumption.

The Greek tradition of "philoxenia", love of strangers, or hospitality, creates sufficiency through generosity rather than accumulation. In traditional Greek island communities, wealth was measured not by what one hoarded but by one's capacity to welcome others. A family was considered prosperous when they could feed unexpected guests without anxiety, not when they possessed the largest house. This framework inverts contemporary wealth signaling; sufficiency demonstrates itself through giving rather than having. Anthropologist Michael Herzfeld documented how Cretan shepherds in the 1980s would compete not over flock size but over who could provide more generous hospitality, creating what he termed "agonistic generosity," a form of status competition that distributed rather than concentrated resources.

The Spanish concept of "sobremesa", the time spent lingering at the table after a meal, represents temporal rather than material sufficiency. In cultures where sobremesa is valued, enough time has been allocated to eating when conversation flows naturally, when digestion can occur leisurely, and when the social bonds that make life meaningful are reinforced. This stands in stark contrast to efficiency-oriented cultures where meals become fuel stops, optimized for speed rather than satisfaction. The difference isn't simply a matter of preference but reflects fundamentally different frameworks for evaluating time sufficiency: Is enough time the minimum required to accomplish a task, or the amount that allows the task to serve its deeper purposes?

Corporate Appropriation and the Commercialization of Sufficiency

The irony of contemporary sufficiency discourse is how rapidly market forces have commodified the very principles meant to resist commodification. "Minimalism" has become a consumer aesthetic that requires specific products: the perfectly curated capsule wardrobe of expensive basics, the Instagram-worthy bare apartment with designer furniture, and the premium meditation app. Marie Kondo's "KonMari" method sparked a decluttering movement that simultaneously generated enormous sales of storage containers, organizational systems, and replacement items that "spark joy." This represents perhaps the ultimate achievement of consumer capitalism: selling sufficiency itself as a product requiring ongoing purchases.

The wellness industry exemplifies this paradox. Traditional Buddhist meditation practices, developed specifically to reduce attachment and desire, are now marketed as productivity tools requiring expensive retreats, apps, cushions, and accessories. Yoga, emerging from philosophical frameworks centered on non-attachment, generates a $37 billion industry in the United States alone. Forest bathing, the Japanese practice of "shinrin-yoku", has spawned guidebooks, workshops, and certified instructors for what originally meant simply spending time among trees. Even radical sufficiency movements like voluntary simplicity generate markets: tiny house construction has become a boutique industry, with custom builds costing over $100,000, hardly simple or accessible.

This commercial appropriation doesn't necessarily negate the underlying principles, but it does reveal how cultural frameworks get absorbed and transformed. When sufficiency becomes an identity or aesthetic requiring specific consumption patterns, it loses its fundamental challenge to consumption logic itself.

Chapter 4: The Economics of Enough

The discipline of economics, despite its mathematical veneer and claim to scientific objectivity, rests on a premise so fundamental that economists rarely examine it: human wants are infinite while resources are finite. This assumption, formally known as the problem of scarcity, drives every model, every policy recommendation, every market mechanism that shapes modern life. Yet this foundational premise contains a hidden logical flaw that becomes apparent when examined closely: if human wants were truly infinite, the concept of satisfaction would be psychologically impossible, rendering the entire notion of utility maximization, the cornerstone of economic theory, incoherent. An infinite want can never be satisfied, even partially, much less maximized. The entire edifice of modern economics implicitly assumes that human wants are extensive but ultimately finite, and that people have a threshold beyond which additional consumption provides negligible benefit. In other words, mainstream economics covertly depends on the existence of "enough" while simultaneously building systems that deny its relevance. This contradiction creates economic structures that produce material abundance while engineering perpetual dissatisfaction, generating unprecedented wealth while corroding the capacity to determine when we have sufficient wealth. Understanding this paradox requires examining how economic systems actively construct and reconstruct the boundaries of enough, transforming what should be a stable point of sufficiency into a constantly receding horizon.

The Industrial Revolution fundamentally altered humanity's relationship with sufficiency by introducing production capacities that, for the first time in history, could exceed basic human needs. Before industrialization, most economic activity focused on subsistence, producing enough food, shelter, and basic goods to survive. Markets existed, luxuries circulated among elites, but the vast majority of human economic effort aimed at sufficiency rather than surplus. The mechanization of production disrupted this equation by creating output that dramatically exceeded basic requirements. This surplus created what economic historians call the "realization problem": how to convert potential production into actual consumption when fundamental needs were already met. The solution, developed gradually across the nineteenth and twentieth centuries, involved manufacturing new needs through advertising, planned obsolescence, and social status competition. Economist Thorstein Veblen, writing in 1899, identified "conspicuous consumption" purchasing goods primarily to signal social standing rather than to meet functional requirements, as a defining feature of the emerging industrial economy. What Veblen observed was the birth of a new economic logic: rather than economies serving to meet established population needs, populations would need to expand their needs to sustain economic production continuously. This inversion, from production serving consumption to consumption serving production, represents one of the most profound and under-examined transformations in human economic organization.

The Growth Imperative and the Sufficiency Problem

Contemporary economic systems operate under what economist Herman Daly termed the "growth imperative", the requirement that economies must perpetually expand to remain healthy. This imperative stems from multiple structural features: debt-based monetary systems that require future growth to service present obligations, employment structures that depend on expanding output to absorb workforce growth, and investment mechanisms that require continuous returns to maintain capital flows. A "steady-state economy", one that maintains stable throughput of materials and energy while sustaining quality of life, appears in this framework as economic stagnation, a crisis to be avoided through stimulus and intervention. The problem becomes apparent when we recognize that perpetual growth on a finite planet constitutes a mathematical impossibility. Even assuming infinite substitutability of resources and perfect recycling efficiency, assumptions that violate physical laws, exponential growth eventually collides with absolute boundaries. The growth imperative thus creates a structural antagonism toward sufficiency: an economic system requiring perpetual expansion cannot accommodate the concept of "enough" without experiencing crisis.

This antagonism manifests in measurable ways. Research by economist Juliet Schor at Boston College demonstrates that average American working hours increased significantly between 1973 and 2000, despite productivity gains that, in theory, could have maintained 1973 living standards while reducing work time by 30%. Instead, productivity gains translated almost entirely into increased consumption rather than increased leisure. Workers ran faster on the treadmill to afford more goods rather than stepping off to maintain their existing standard of living. This pattern reveals a crucial insight: economic systems channel productivity gains toward expanding consumption rather than achieving sufficiency more efficiently. The question "Could we maintain current well-being while working less and consuming less?" remains unasked mainly within mainstream economics because the answer, almost certainly yes, would undermine the growth imperative. Countries like the Netherlands and Denmark, where average working hours are 25-30% lower than in the United States while maintaining comparable living standards and higher reported well-being scores, provide empirical evidence that sufficiency-oriented economics can function in practice. Yet these examples are typically dismissed as culturally specific rather than examined as alternative models, because acknowledging their viability would require confronting uncomfortable questions about whose interests the growth imperative serves.

The measurement systems economics employs further obscures the sufficiency question. Gross Domestic Product (GDP), the primary metric for economic health, measures throughput rather than welfare, activity rather than achievement. GDP increases when we purchase medication to treat illness, when we rebuild after natural disasters, and when we buy solutions to problems our consumption patterns created. Italian economist Lorenzo Fioramonti notes that GDP treats a nation as healthier when citizens are treating cancer than when they are healthy, more prosperous when they are rebuilding flood-damaged homes than when those homes remain intact. This measurement framework creates what philosophers call a category error, assessing system health through a metric that measures system activity, regardless of whether that activity enhances or degrades well-being. The Genuine Progress Indicator (GPI), developed by ecological economists, attempts to correct this by accounting for costs like environmental degradation, resource depletion, and income inequality. Studies comparing GDP and GPI across multiple nations reveal a striking pattern: while GDP has risen continuously since 1970, GPI peaked in most developed nations around 1975-1980 and has since stagnated or declined. This divergence suggests that economic growth beyond a certain threshold may generate activity and profit without improving, and possibly while actively degrading, actual human welfare.

Market Mechanisms and the Manufacture of Insufficiency

Market economies deploy sophisticated mechanisms that actively prevent individuals from reaching stable points of sufficiency. The fashion industry provides an obvious example of how markets manufacture inadequacy. Clothing production more than doubled between 2000 and 2015, while average wear-per-garment decreased by 36%, according to data from the Ellen MacArthur Foundation. This acceleration didn't result from spontaneous consumer desire but from systematic industry restructuring. Fast-fashion brands like Zara and H&M pioneered business models based on rapid inventory turnover, introducing new designs weekly rather than seasonally, training consumers to view clothing as having dramatically shorter useful lives. The economic logic is straightforward: a consumer who wears a coat for 10 years counts as one sale, while a consumer who replaces a coat annually counts as 10 sales in the same category. Markets, therefore, reward strategies that accelerate replacement cycles, rendering perfectly functional goods psychologically obsolete through style changes, social signaling, or subtle quality degradation. This dynamic extends far beyond fashion, smartphone upgrade cycles, automobile model refreshes, home decor trends, and even food fashions follow similar patterns of planned psychological obsolescence.

The financial services industry has developed another mechanism for preventing sufficiency: expanding the definition of necessary financial products. In 1970, a typical American household might maintain a checking account, a savings account, and perhaps a mortgage. By 2020, the same household would be considered financially unsophisticated without credit cards, retirement accounts (potentially multiple, including 401k, IRA, and Roth IRA), 529 education savings plans, health savings accounts, life insurance, disability insurance, umbrella liability insurance, and various investment vehicles. Each product addresses a genuine risk or opportunity, yet collectively they create an ever-expanding frontier of financial preparation that makes sufficiency perpetually elusive. Financial literacy programs, ostensibly designed to help citizens manage money effectively, typically define literacy as competent participation in this expanding system rather than questioning whether such complexity serves individual well-being. Economic anthropologist David Graeber argued that financialization, the increasing dominance of financial services in the economy, requires creating a sense of perpetual anxiety about future needs as a precondition for selling increasingly elaborate financial products. A person confident they have enough savings is a problem for an industry built on managing inadequacy.

The housing market demonstrates how economic mechanisms can transform sufficiency into a receding target through the interaction of speculation and positional competition. When homes function primarily as shelter, sufficiency has a relatively straightforward definition: adequate space for household members, decent condition, and reasonable location relative to employment and services. However, when housing becomes a primary wealth-building asset, as financial advisors routinely recommend, the calculus changes fundamentally. A home that serves shelter needs perfectly may nonetheless be "insufficient" if it isn't appreciating adequately, isn't in a neighborhood with competitive school rankings, or doesn't provide the equity extraction necessary for retirement planning. Real estate economist Edward Glaeser's research reveals that housing prices in major metropolitan areas are increasingly disconnected from construction costs, instead reflecting positional competition for access to high-performing school districts, proximity to employment centers, and neighborhood status signaling. This transformation means that housing sufficiency is no longer determined by the physical structure's capacity to shelter but by its position in multiple overlapping competitive hierarchies. The result is that median-income families in cities like San Francisco, Boston, or Vancouver find themselves perpetually housing-insufficient, not because adequate physical shelter is unavailable but because adequate positional access has become economically unreachable.

Alternative Economic Frameworks and the Sufficiency Threshold

A small but growing body of economic thought challenges the growth imperative by centering sufficiency as an explicit goal. Kate Raworth's "Doughnut Economics" model proposes an economic framework bounded by two boundaries: a social foundation below which human needs are unmet, and an ecological ceiling beyond which environmental systems are degraded. Between these boundaries lies a safe and just space for humanity, an area where sufficiency is achieved for all while maintaining ecological integrity. Raworth's model inverts conventional economic thinking by defining the goal not as maximizing throughput but as achieving sustainable adequacy. The implementation of doughnut economics principles in cities like Amsterdam and Copenhagen has revealed both the model's potential and the structural barriers to a sufficiency-based economy. Amsterdam's municipal government used the framework to redesign procurement policies, urban planning decisions, and economic development strategies around sufficiency thresholds. Early results show reduced material consumption without corresponding declines in well-being indicators, suggesting that sufficiency-oriented policy can maintain quality of life while reducing throughput. However, these experiments also revealed how deeply growth-oriented assumptions are embedded in everything from tax policy to zoning regulations to education curricula.

The concept of "degrowth", voluntary economic contraction in wealthy nations to achieve ecological sustainability and improved well-being, represents another challenge to conventional financial wisdom. Degrowth economist Giorgos Kallis argues that rich countries have exceeded the threshold at which additional economic growth generates meaningful improvements in wellbeing and should therefore intentionally contract material throughput while expanding non-market sources of satisfaction: community relationships, creative activity, political participation, and ecological engagement. Critics dismiss degrowth as politically naive or economically catastrophic, arguing that contraction would inevitably cause unemployment, poverty, and social instability. However, research by ecological economist Peter Victor using macroeconomic modeling suggests that managed degrowth scenarios, combining reduced working hours, income redistribution, increased public services, and cancellation of household debt, could reduce environmental impact while maintaining or improving wellbeing indicators and avoiding an economic crisis. The key term is "managed" degrowth, which differs from recession in being intentional, equitable, and designed to maintain social welfare while reducing throughput. Whether such management is politically feasible remains an open question, but the models demonstrate that sufficiency-based economics is not mathematically impossible; rather, it is structurally challenging given current institutional arrangements.

Some economists argue that technology will resolve the tension between growth imperatives and finite resources through dematerialization, delivering greater value with fewer physical inputs. The information economy, where value often inheres in software, design, and data rather than physical goods, supposedly proves that economic growth can decouple from material consumption. However, this optimistic assessment overlooks what researchers call the "rebound effect": efficiency improvements typically enable consumption increases that partially or entirely offset material savings. More fuel-efficient vehicles, for instance, make driving cheaper, leading people to drive more; the net impact on fuel consumption is often minimal. Physicist Vaclav Smil's comprehensive analysis of dematerialization claims reveals a sobering pattern. While individual products have become more materially efficient, aggregate material consumption continues rising because product proliferation and consumption expansion exceed per-unit efficiency gains. The smartphone revolution provides a telling example: individual devices contain far less material than the desktop computers, cameras, GPS devices, and other electronics they replaced, yet total material flows from electronics manufacturing have increased dramatically because smartphone penetration now exceeds 80% of the global population, replacement cycles average 2-3 years, and the cloud infrastructure supporting smartphone functionality requires enormous data centers consuming massive energy and material resources.

The economic challenge of sufficiency ultimately centers on a question that sounds simple but proves extraordinarily difficult to address systematically: How much material throughput is required to sustain a genuinely high quality of life for a given population? Research by ecological economists identifies what they call the "sufficient wellbeing threshold," the level of resource consumption beyond which additional consumption provides minimal wellbeing gains. Studies consistently place this threshold significantly below current consumption levels in wealthy nations but well above the global average. The implication is stark: achieving global sufficiency would require wealthy nations to consume less while poor nations consume more, with the transition managed to avoid economic disruption. This redistribution faces not just political resistance but structural barriers embedded in economic systems designed to perpetuate rather than resolve inequality. Interest-bearing debt, for instance, mathematically requires perpetual growth to avoid crisis, as economist Richard Werner's work demonstrates. Similarly, pension systems and insurance mechanisms depend on investment returns that assume perpetual expansion. Restructuring these systems to function within sufficiency constraints would require institutional transformations that threaten powerful interests, which explains why sufficiency-based economics remains marginal despite its logical coherence and empirical support.

Understanding the economics of enough reveals that our apparent inability to feel satisfied is not a personal failing but a structural feature of economic systems that require perpetual expansion to function. These systems actively manufacture dissatisfaction, not through conspiracy but through the ordinary operation of market mechanisms, growth imperatives, and measurement systems that confuse activity with achievement. Recognizing this dynamic doesn't immediately resolve the sufficiency problem; the institutional barriers are real and formidable, but it reframes the challenge. The question is not "Why can't I feel satisfied despite having so much?" but "How can I recognize sufficiency within a system designed to make sufficiency impossible?" The answer requires both individual strategies for resisting manufactured insufficiency and collective efforts to restructure economic institutions around sustainable adequacy rather than perpetual expansion. The stakes extend beyond personal well-being to ecological survival: an economic system incapable of recognizing enough is on a collision course with planetary boundaries. The economics of enough, properly understood, is not a niche concern for ascetics and philosophers but the central economic challenge of our era.

The Psychology of Economic Sufficiency

The structural barriers to sufficiency-based economics are reinforced by psychological mechanisms that economists have only recently begun to examine seriously. Behavioral economists like Daniel Kahneman have documented how individuals systematically misjudge their future satisfaction, a phenomenon known as "affective forecasting error." People consistently overestimate how much happiness a purchase will bring and how long that happiness will last, while underestimating how quickly they will adapt to new possessions and return to their baseline level of satisfaction. This adaptation process, sometimes called the "hedonic treadmill," means that material improvements provide temporary satisfaction boosts that fade as circumstances return to normal. A promotion that initially feels transformative becomes ordinary within months; a new home that seemed perfect soon reveals inadequacies; a salary that once seemed lavish eventually feels merely adequate as lifestyle adjusts upward to match income.

What makes this pattern economically significant is that markets systematically exploit these forecasting errors. Advertising doesn't sell products so much as it sells anticipated satisfaction, the promise of how you'll feel when you own something, rather than a realistic assessment of the satisfaction duration. Marketing research has long understood that desire is more profitable than satisfaction: a satisfied customer may not purchase again, but a desiring customer represents an ongoing revenue opportunity. This creates what economist Tibor Scitovsky termed "joyless economies", systems that excel at stimulating desire while structurally undermining the capacity for satisfaction. The economic incentive structure favors keeping consumers in a state of perpetual wanting rather than helping them achieve stable contentment, because contentment represents market exit while wanting represents continued engagement.

Chapter 5: Minimalism and the Art of Letting Go

The relationship between human beings and their possessions carries an invisible weight that becomes perceptible only when we begin removing items from our lives. A closet crowded with clothing demands not just physical space but cognitive bandwidth, decisions about what to wear, maintenance routines, organizational systems, and the low-level anxiety that accompanies disorder. Remove half the contents, and something unexpected occurs: the remaining items become more visible, more valued, more frequently worn. This paradox, that subtraction can increase both utility and satisfaction, sits at the heart of minimalism's psychological potency. Yet minimalism is persistently misunderstood as an aesthetic preference for sparse interiors or an extreme lifestyle choice involving tiny houses and capsule wardrobes. These visible manifestations obscure minimalism's more profound significance: it represents a systematic methodology for identifying and eliminating the excess that masks what genuinely matters. The art of letting go is not about deprivation but about clarity, not about having less but about making room for enough to become sufficient.

Contemporary minimalism emerged from multiple tributaries, including Japanese aesthetic traditions, American countercultural movements, and environmental consciousness. What distinguishes current minimalist practice from simple frugality or asceticism is its emphasis on intentionality rather than scarcity. Minimalist practitioners are not necessarily spending less money or living in smaller spaces than their peers; they are making different calculations about what deserves inclusion in their lives. The minimalist asks not "Can I afford this?" but "Does this serve a purpose significant enough to justify the space, maintenance, attention, and psychological burden it will require?" This reframing transforms acquisition from a default response to a deliberate choice. Architect Ludwig Mies van der Rohe's dictum "less is more" captures this inversion: reducing elements can amplify impact rather than diminish it. A room containing three carefully chosen objects generates more aesthetic and emotional resonance than one crowded with thirty items competing for attention. This principle extends beyond physical spaces into schedules, relationships, commitments, and information streams. The art of letting go involves recognizing that every yes contains an implicit no, accepting one opportunity means declining others, and that indiscriminate accumulation prevents the concentration necessary for mastery or deep satisfaction.

The neuroscience underlying minimalism's effectiveness reveals why decluttering can produce such disproportionate psychological relief. The visual cortex allocates processing resources to everything in the visual field, so cluttered environments create a constant low-level cognitive load as the brain processes, categorizes, and tracks numerous objects. Research by Princeton University neuroscientists Sabine Kastner and Stephen McMains demonstrates that multiple stimuli present in the visual field mutually suppress their neural representations, degrading the brain's ability to process any single stimulus effectively. Decluttered environments don't merely look cleaner; they actually allow the brain to process remaining stimuli with greater clarity and less interference. This finding helps explain the common experience of feeling mentally clearer in organized spaces, even when we're not consciously aware of the disorder. The effect extends to digital environments: research on information overload shows that cluttered computer desktops, overflowing email inboxes, and excessive browser tabs create measurable cognitive drag. The brain treats digital items similarly to physical ones, allocating attention and working memory to track and categorize them. The person who maintains two hundred browser tabs open simultaneously is not maximizing information access but instead fragmenting attention so thoroughly that deep engagement with any single information source becomes nearly impossible.

The Sunk Cost Fallacy and Possession Liberation

One of the most potent psychological barriers to letting go is what economists call the sunk cost fallacy, the tendency to continue investing in something we've already invested in, regardless of whether that investment serves our interests. This cognitive bias extends beyond financial decisions into our relationship with possessions. An expensive piece of exercise equipment sits unused in a garage, but we can't donate it because "we paid good money for it." A degree we regret pursuing binds us to a career path we find unfulfilling because abandoning it would mean "wasting" years of study. Clothing with tags still attached fills closets because discarding unworn items would require acknowledging poor purchasing decisions. The sunk cost fallacy transforms past mistakes into present burdens by making the remedy, letting go, feel like compounding the error. Economist Richard Thaler's research on mental accounting reveals that we psychologically categorize identical monetary losses differently depending on how we frame them. Money spent on an item that proved disappointing feels like a smaller loss if we keep the item than if we discard it, even though the money is equally gone in both scenarios, and the kept item actively diminishes our quality of life.

Overcoming the sunk cost fallacy requires cognitive reframing that separates past decisions from present reality.

The purchase price of an unused item is already spent; the only remaining question is whether keeping or releasing it better serves our current needs. This distinction between honoring past choices and being imprisoned by them proves surprisingly difficult for most people. Japanese organizing consultant Fumio Sasaki describes his experience maintaining an extensive book collection not because he read the books, but because discarding them would require admitting he would never read them, an acknowledgment his self-concept as an intellectual resisted. The books represented not current value but aspirational identity, and releasing them meant releasing that identity. When he finally began donating books, Sasaki experienced what he describes as a psychological liberation disproportionate to the physical space recovered. The books had been consuming mental space through guilt, obligation, and the perpetual low-level reminder of unfulfilled intentions. Letting them go eliminated not just physical clutter but psychological debt.

The endowment effect, our tendency to overvalue things merely because we own them, further complicates letting go. Research by behavioral economists Daniel Kahneman, Jack Knetsch, and Richard Thaler demonstrated that people demand significantly more money to sell an object they own than they would pay to acquire an identical object they don't own. This asymmetry suggests that ownership itself creates value independent of the object's utility. The endowment effect helps explain why decluttering proves emotionally difficult even when we intellectually recognize that items serve no purpose. The coffee mug we never use feels different from an identical mug in a store; ours carries the intangible value of belonging to us. Minimalist practice deliberately counteracts the endowment effect by regularly reassessing possessions against functional and emotional utility rather than allowing ownership to become a reason for keeping things. Some minimalists practice "container limits", deciding that clothing must fit in a single closet, books must fit on existing shelves, and kitchen implements must fit in designated drawers. When new items arrive, old items must leave to maintain the container limit. This creates a forcing function that prevents accumulation through the passive endowment effect.

The Identity-Possession Entanglement

Possessions carry symbolic weight that extends far beyond their functional value, serving as physical manifestations of identity, memories, and aspirations. A wedding dress worn once but kept for decades represents not fabric but an identity marker: "person who had that wedding, that relationship, that life stage." Children's artwork covering refrigerators symbolizes "devoted parent." Collections, whether of vinyl records, vintage cameras, or sports memorabilia, communicate enthusiast identity to ourselves and others. This symbolic dimension means that letting go of possessions can feel like eroding identity itself. Anthropologist Daniel Miller's research on material culture reveals how objects serve as what he calls "objectification", making abstract relationships and identities concrete and tangible. A teenager's bedroom decorations are not just aesthetic choices but identity claims, saying "this is who I am" in a developmental stage where self-concept remains fluid and uncertain. Adults engage in similar identity-possession entanglement but often more subtly: the home gym equipment says "I am athletic," the musical instrument "I am creative," the professional library "I am intellectual."

The challenge arises when possessions represent aspirational rather than actual identity, who we wish we were rather than who we are. The guitar sitting unplayed for five years represents not current musicianship but the identity claim "I am the kind of person who plays guitar." Letting it go requires acknowledging the gap between aspiration and reality and accepting that we are not that person, at least not currently. This acknowledgment can feel like diminishment rather than clarification. Yet identity-possession entanglement creates a subtle trap: accumulating symbols of aspirational identities can substitute for actually developing those identities. The person who buys painting supplies but never paints, exercise equipment but never exercises, or cookbooks but never cooks is engaging in what psychologists call "identity signaling," that paradoxically reduces the probability of actual identity development. The purchased items create the feeling of progress; I'm becoming a painter, an athlete, a chef, without requiring the sustained effort those identities demand. Minimalist practitioners often report that releasing aspirational items paradoxically freed them to either genuinely pursue those activities or acknowledge that they didn't actually want to, reducing the psychological burden of perpetually unfulfilled intentions.

Memories present a particularly complex entanglement. Objects serve as memory anchors, a concert ticket, a souvenir from a meaningful trip, or a gift from someone important. These items carry minimal functional value but enormous emotional weight as physical connections to experiences and relationships. The fear that discarding the object will erase or dishonor the memory creates powerful resistance to letting go. Yet memory research reveals this fear is largely unfounded. Cognitive psychologist Linda Henkel's work on the "photo-taking impairment effect" demonstrates that the presence of external memory aids can actually weaken the formation of internal memory. People who photograph museum exhibits extensively remember them less well than those who observe them, suggesting that external anchors can substitute for rather than supplement internal memory. Similarly, keeping every memento from a meaningful relationship or experience may provide a comforting sense of preservation while actually outsourcing memory to objects, thereby weakening our internal recollection. Some minimalists practice photographing items before releasing them, creating a digital record that serves as a memory aid without the physical burden. Others keep only a single representative item from categories, one piece of childhood artwork rather than every drawing, one ticket stub from a meaningful concert series rather than every ticket. These practices acknowledge memory's legitimate importance while recognizing that meaningful recollection doesn't require comprehensive physical documentation.

The Liberation-Grief Paradox

Letting go generates contradictory emotions that can coexist uncomfortably: relief at reducing burden alongside grief at losing something that once held meaning. This simultaneity confuses many people attempting decluttering, who expect to feel uniformly lighter and instead experience waves of sadness, guilt, or regret interspersed with the anticipated liberation. The presence of negative emotions leads them to conclude they're making mistakes or being too extreme, often halting the process before reaching the psychological clarity that emerges on the other side of the grief. Understanding that letting go is a legitimate loss, even when it's a beneficial one, helps normalize the emotional complexity. Grief counselor Kenneth Doka's work on "disenfranchised grief" identifies losses that society doesn't typically recognize as legitimate grief occasions: the end of a job we disliked, moving from a house we'd outgrown, or the death of an estranged relative. Discarding possessions represents disenfranchised grief; we're supposed to feel only relief, making the sadness feel inappropriate or weak. Yet the items we release often carry hopes, memories, or self-concepts, and their departure deserves acknowledgment.

The Japanese concept of "mono no aware", the pathos of things, offers a framework for honoring this complexity. It describes the bittersweet recognition of impermanence, the gentle sadness of acknowledging that all things, including our relationships with objects, are transitory. Items that served us well and are now departing deserve gratitude and a conscious goodbye rather than casual disposal. Some minimalist practitioners create small rituals around significant releases: thanking an item for its service, acknowledging what it represented, and consciously releasing it rather than simply throwing it away. Marie Kondo's controversial practice of thanking objects before discarding them drew mockery, but addresses a genuine psychological need. The ritual creates space for acknowledging the loss while affirming the choice to let go. It transforms disposal from rejection into grateful release, changing the emotional valence without changing the physical action. Whether one literally thanks objects matters less than creating some form of conscious closure rather than treating letting go as purely mechanical sorting.

The liberation that emerges after working through this grief-relief paradox often surprises people with its intensity. Many minimalist practitioners describe experiencing unexpected cognitive and emotional expansion after substantial decluttering. The sense of possibility increases, freed from managing, organizing, and navigating around numerous possessions, they discover bandwidth for activities and relationships that had felt impossible within their previous constrained life. Psychologist Mihaly Csikszentmihalyi's research on "flow states", complete immersion in engaging activities, identifies that flow requires both clear goals and immediate, unobstructed feedback. Cluttered, complex environments create constant low-level distraction that prevents the mental clarity necessary for flow. Minimalist environments don't automatically create flow, but they remove barriers to it, making deep engagement more accessible. This connects to the concept of "decision fatigue", the progressive deterioration of decision quality after making numerous decisions. Psychologist Roy Baumeister's research demonstrates that decision-making consumes a limited cognitive resource, meaning that trivial decisions about which coffee mug to use or which clothes to wear deplete the same resource needed for significant decisions. Minimalist practice reduces trivial decision load by limiting options, preserving cognitive resources for decisions that genuinely matter.

Practical Systems for Sustainable Minimalism

The challenge most people encounter is not initial decluttering but preventing reaccumulation. Possessions flow into our lives through numerous channels, gifts, purchases, free items, work materials, children's belongings, inherited items, and without systematic barriers, they accumulate regardless of our intentions. The most effective minimalist systems focus less on one-time purges and more on establishing ongoing practices that regulate inflow and outflow. The "one in, one out" rule, bringing in a new item only when releasing an existing one, creates a steady-state system that prevents accumulation while allowing refreshment and replacement. This simple heuristic short-circuits the acquisition impulse by making it explicitly consequential; buying new running shoes means choosing which existing shoes to donate. The forced-choice question makes us confront whether the new item genuinely represents an improvement or merely novelty.

Waiting periods before purchases create friction that allows impulse to subside and rational evaluation to emerge. Some minimalists practice a 30-day waiting list: any desired item is added to a list with a date, and the purchase proceeds only if the desire persists for 30 days. Research by marketing professor David Bell on impulse purchasing reveals that the majority of impulse purchases are regretted within a week, suggesting that even brief delays would prevent significant unnecessary purchases. The waiting period accomplishes multiple psychological functions: it allows the neurochemical spike of wanting to dissipate, permits research and comparison that might reveal better alternatives or the item's actual inadequacy, and creates space for recognizing that we already own something similar. The digital age makes immediate purchasing dangerously frictionless, and one-click ordering removes all deliberation space between desire and ownership. Deliberately reintroducing friction counteracts this engineered impulsivity.

Regular decluttering cycles prevent the overwhelming accumulation that makes letting go feel impossible. Rather than waiting until clutter reaches crisis proportions, systematic minimalists schedule quarterly or semiannual reviews to reassess possessions against current needs and values. This practice acknowledges that sufficiency is not static; what served us well last year may no longer serve us now, and our relationships with objects appropriately evolve. The person who needed an extensive professional wardrobe but has transitioned to remote work no longer needs those items; keeping them wastes space and prevents someone else from using them. The family whose children have grown no longer needs toys, sports equipment, or themed bedroom decorations. Regular reviews create permission to release items that served their purpose and are now complete, rather than treating all possessions as permanent commitments.

Some practitioners find that seasonal changes provide natural review opportunities; the transition to summer makes winter coat excess apparent, while fall prompts reassessment of summer recreation equipment.

The concept of "exit pathways" addresses the practical friction that prevents letting go even when we've decided items should go. Many people accumulate piles of items marked "donate" that sit for months or years because actually completing the donation requires effort: finding appropriate organizations, confirming donation hours, transporting items, and obtaining receipts. This friction converts the emotional work of letting go into an incomplete action that clutters space while generating guilt. Establishing specific, minimal-friction exit pathways makes letting go logistically practical. This might involve: identifying a regular donation pickup service that requires only leaving items on the porch, maintaining a permanent "donation box" near the door that prompts immediate placement rather than pile creation, or scheduling quarterly donation trips on the calendar like any other commitment. For items with resale value, establishing a clear protocol, "if not sold within two weeks of listing, automatically donate", prevents the limbo of items semi-released but not actually gone. The goal is to make the exit so frictionless that the emotional decision to let go can translate immediately into physical release.

The relationship between minimalism and "enough" becomes most apparent when we recognize that excess prevents us from recognizing sufficiency. The person surrounded by options paradoxically experiences all of them as inadequate; with so many choices, surely the perfect one exists just beyond reach. The wardrobe containing forty shirts makes getting dressed daily frustrating because too many mediocre options obscure the few excellent ones. The kitchen, crowded with specialized gadgets, makes cooking more complex rather than simpler. The digital library of thousands of unread books creates guilt rather than possibility. Minimalist practice removes the excess that obscures enough, allowing us to recognize and inhabit sufficiency. This doesn't require an extreme reduction, but rather one that brings the remaining items to a point where they are genuinely valued and used. The precise number varies from person to person; what constitutes minimalism for one person might feel cluttered to another or sparse to a third. The relevant question is not "Do I own fewer than X items?" but rather "Do I value and utilize what I own, and does it serve my actual life rather than an aspirational identity or past version of myself?" When we can answer yes, we've achieved the functional clarity that minimalism promises, not through deprivation but through the art of letting go.

Chapter 6: Enough in Personal Relationships

The architecture of human intimacy operates according to principles that directly contradict the additive logic governing most other areas of contemporary life. While career success often correlates with expanding professional networks, and financial security involves accumulating resources, relational depth emerges through selective concentration rather than expansive collection. A person maintaining fifty casual friendships typically experiences less emotional sustenance than one cultivating five intimate connections. A couple attempting to keep alive every acquaintance from their past while constantly forming new social bonds often finds their partnership suffering from attention deficit. This peculiar mathematics of intimacy, where addition usually produces subtraction, and strategic reduction generates multiplication of satisfaction, makes relationships perhaps the most counterintuitive domain for applying the concept of enough. The question "How many relationships are sufficient?" appears almost obscene in a culture that treats social connection as universally beneficial, where "networking" functions as both verb and virtue, and where social media platforms measure our worth by accumulator metrics: followers, friends, connections, contacts. Yet anyone who has experienced the exhaustion of maintaining relationships beyond their genuine capacity, or felt the hollowness of conversations distributed too thinly across too many people, intuitively recognizes that relational sufficiency involves boundaries most of us have never consciously established.

What makes relational sufficiency particularly challenging is that relationships, unlike possessions or commitments, involve other conscious beings with their own expectations, needs, and definitions of adequate attention. You can discard an unworn jacket without negotiation, but withdrawing energy from a friendship requires navigating hurt feelings, social judgment, and your own guilt. The coat doesn't feel rejected; the friend might. This emotional complexity causes many people to maintain relationships beyond the point where they provide mutual nourishment, creating what relationship researcher Shasta Nelson calls "frientimacy deficit disorder", the condition of having many connections but few that deliver genuine intimacy, vulnerability, or meaningful reciprocity. The person with three hundred Facebook friends who feels profoundly lonely on Friday evening isn't suffering from insufficient connections but from inadequate depth, having distributed their limited relational energy so broadly that no individual relationship receives sufficient investment to become truly sustaining. The remedy involves not addition but subtraction and concentration, a prescription that feels emotionally threatening even when intellectually obvious.

The Ecology of Attention in Intimate Partnerships

Romantic partnerships reveal, with particular clarity, how the question of enough extends beyond the relationship itself into how partners allocate attention across all life domains. Therapist Esther Perel observes that modern couples face an unprecedented challenge: they expect their partnership to simultaneously provide passionate romance, deep friendship, co-parenting partnership, financial collaboration, and personal identity affirmation, while both partners often maintain career demands, social obligations, family responsibilities, and personal pursuits that previous generations rarely attempted to balance simultaneously. The mathematics doesn't work. If career demands claim 50 hours weekly, children require 40 hours, extended family obligations take 10 hours, personal fitness and health management need 8 hours, and basic life maintenance consumes another 20 hours, the 168-hour weekly budget leaves 40 hours for sleep and partnership combined. Even if sleep receives minimal allocation, the couple shares perhaps twenty-five hours weekly, less time than either might spend in meetings. This attention budget renders the romantic ideal of "never stop dating your spouse" mathematically absurd unless other commitments are substantially reduced.

The concept of relational sufficiency in partnerships, therefore, cannot be separated from the larger question of life sufficiency. Partners often approach the relationship asking, "Are you giving me enough attention?" when the more productive question might be, "Have we jointly defined what constitutes enough in all domains so that our partnership receives adequate resource allocation within sustainable constraints?" This reframing transforms the problem from individual deficiency to systemic design. Research by sociologist Arlie Hochschild on "time bind" dynamics shows that couples often unconsciously allow work to expand indefinitely precisely because workplace achievement offers more precise metrics and more immediate feedback than relational investment. A completed project delivers concrete satisfaction; an evening of undistracted conversation with one's partner yields ambiguous returns that may not feel rewarding in real time, even while contributing fundamentally to long-term relational health. The result is a systematic underinvestment in partnership, not because individuals don't value the relationship, but because they lack frameworks for defining adequate investment and protecting that allocation against perpetual encroachment from domains with more urgent apparent demands.

Some couples attempting to address this challenge adopt what family therapist Terry Real calls "relational minimums", explicitly negotiated agreements about baseline attention allocations the partnership requires to remain vital. One couple might establish that three uninterrupted dinners weekly and one extended conversation on weekends constitute their relational minimum; another might define sufficient connection as twenty minutes of morning coffee together and one date afternoon monthly. The specific content matters far less than the act of conscious definition and mutual agreement. These negotiations force couples to confront questions typically left implicit: What do we actually need from each other to feel adequately connected? What constitutes enough attention, enough romance, enough practical support, enough emotional availability? The discomfort these conversations generate reveals how thoroughly we avoid defining relational sufficiency, perhaps because doing so requires acknowledging that we cannot provide everything our partner might want. They cannot provide everything we might desire. Establishing "enough" means simultaneously accepting limits, a psychologically threatening acknowledgment in a culture that insists love should be limitless.

The Friendship Paradox and Dunbar's Number

Anthropologist Robin Dunbar's research on primate social structures suggests that human cognitive capacity supports approximately 150 stable relationships, the number at which individuals can maintain awareness of who everyone is and how they relate to each other. Within this outer boundary, Dunbar identifies concentric circles of intimacy: an inner core of three to five individuals with whom we maintain extremely close bonds, a sympathy group of twelve to fifteen people we turn to for support and confide in regularly, a friendship band of about fifty people we socialize with periodically, and then the outer layer reaching toward 150 comprising acquaintances we recognize and could potentially activate for specific purposes. This architecture suggests that human relational capacity isn't infinitely expandable but operates within definite constraints determined by cognitive processing limits, available time, and emotional bandwidth. The implication is profound: every relationship we maintain occupies space in a finite ecosystem, meaning indiscriminate addition necessarily degrades the average depth of all connections.

Yet contemporary social technology actively encourages us to violate these natural constraints. Professional networking platforms suggest we should continually expand our contact lists; social media enables maintaining hundreds of superficial connections while creating the illusion of intimacy through asymmetric information sharing; and cultural narratives about networking as a career necessity pressure us to treat relationship-building as an optimization problem where more is always better. The result is what sociologist Gerald Mollenhorst calls "network turbulence", the condition in which our social networks change so rapidly that few relationships receive sufficient stability to develop depth. Mollenhorst's longitudinal research tracking the same individuals over seven years found that people replaced approximately half their social network during that period, suggesting that many connections exist in a state of perpetual superficiality, never receiving sustained investment long enough to move inward through Dunbar's concentric circles. The person constantly forming new connections while allowing existing relationships to atrophy isn't maximizing their social capital but rather running laterally through the shallow end of the relationship pool, never diving deep enough to access the real benefits, emotional security, genuine reciprocity, and the earned trust that only develops through sustained mutual vulnerability across time.

The friendship paradox emerges from this misalignment: most people have fewer close friends than their friends have, on average. This mathematical phenomenon occurs because highly connected individuals appear in many people's social networks, skewing the average upward. The psychological impact is that most people feel their social connections are inadequate compared to apparent norms, never recognizing that the "norm" is a statistical illusion. This perceived inadequacy often drives further attempts to expand social networks, exactly the wrong response to what is actually a depth deficit rather than a quantity problem. The remedy involves recognizing that friendship sufficiency isn't measured by network size but by whether your inner circles, particularly that core of three to five intimate relationships, contain people with whom you can be genuinely vulnerable, who know your actual self rather than your curated presentation, and who have demonstrated commitment through actions rather than just affinity. A person with two such friendships has sufficient intimate connection; a person with three hundred social media contacts but no one they could call at three in the morning with a real crisis is suffering profound relational poverty despite appearing socially rich.

The Burden of Relational Debt and Strategic Withdrawal

Relationships accumulate debt, not financial but attentional and emotional obligations that grow heavier over time when not actively serviced. The friend you've been meaning to call for six months, the relative whose messages you haven't returned, the former colleague you keep promising to meet for lunch, each represents a small weight in your cognitive load, a minor drain on your mental bandwidth as your brain periodically surfaces the obligation. You push it back down, promising yourself you'll attend to it later. Psychologist Bluma Zeigarnik discovered that uncompleted tasks occupy more mental space than completed ones, and this principle applies forcefully to relational maintenance. The friend you explicitly decided to let the relationship lapse with occupies less mental real estate than the friend you keep intending to reconnect with but never actually do. The former represents closure; the latter represents perpetual incompletion, draining energy without providing connection.

This accumulation of relational debt often results from an inability to reduce social obligations consciously, even when those relationships no longer serve mutual growth or provide genuine satisfaction to either party. We maintain friendships from high school that have long since lost relevance to our current lives; we preserve professional relationships that offered value in previous career stages but contribute nothing to present circumstances; we stay connected to former romantic partners' families despite the relationships themselves having ended years ago. The justification typically involves loyalty, a desire not to hurt feelings, or vague commitments to the importance of maintaining connections. But these preserved relationships exact opportunity costs by consuming attention, time, and emotional energy that might otherwise flow toward connections that actively nourish current life. Clinical psychologist Nedra Glover Tawwab observes that many people experience relief rather than loss when relationships finally end, precisely because the obligation drained more energy than the connection provided. Yet, they needed permission from external circumstances to withdraw rather than proactively choosing strategic reduction.

Strategic withdrawal, the conscious decision to reduce investment in relationships that have ceased serving mutual flourishing, remains culturally taboo. We lack even adequate language for this process; "ghosting" carries negative connotations, "breaking up" applies only to romantic relationships, and we have no widely accepted term for the intentional, respectful reduction of a friendship that has run its natural course. This linguistic absence reflects conceptual poverty: we haven't developed frameworks for thinking about relational sufficiency that include subtraction as a valid and sometimes necessary operation. Yet every gardener knows that thriving gardens require regular pruning, removing growth that competes with desired plants for light, water, and nutrients. The same principle applies to relational ecosystems: strategic pruning creates conditions for remaining relationships to flourish by concentrating limited resources where they yield the most significant mutual benefit. The alternative, attempting to maintain every connection ever formed, produces not abundant connections but rather an overcrowded garden where nothing receives adequate nourishment and everything exists in a state of struggling adequacy rather than genuine thriving.

Parenting, Sufficiency, and the Myth of Quality Time

The parent-child relationship presents unique challenges for applying sufficiency principles because children's needs evolve continuously, cultural expectations around parenting have intensified dramatically, and most parents experience persistent guilt about never providing enough attention, enrichment, or presence. Sociologist Annette Lareau documents the rise of "concerted cultivation", intensive parenting styles characterized by organized activities, constant supervision, and active development of children's talents and skills. This approach contrasts sharply with previous generations' more permissive "natural growth" strategies, where children spent significant unstructured time with peers, entertaining themselves with minimal adult intervention. Research comparing outcomes between these approaches reveals surprising findings: children raised with concerted cultivation show stronger resume-building skills and institutional navigation abilities, but they don't demonstrate superior psychological adjustment, life satisfaction, or relationship quality compared to peers raised with more autonomy and less intensive parental management.

The implication challenges the implicit assumption in contemporary parenting that more parental involvement necessarily produces better outcomes. Beyond certain thresholds, children need reliable attachment figures, adequate supervision for safety, and sufficient resources for health and development. Additional parental inputs yield diminishing returns and may even have adverse effects. Over-involved parents can undermine children's development of autonomy, problem-solving capacity, and resilience by removing obstacles that would otherwise provide valuable learning experiences. Yet "how much parenting is enough?" remains almost impossible to answer definitively because adequacy varies by child temperament, family circumstances, and cultural context. What constitutes sufficient parental presence for a self-directed adolescent differs dramatically from requirements for a young child with developmental challenges. This variability means parents cannot rely on universal formulas. Still, it must instead develop situation-specific definitions of adequate involvement, a cognitively demanding task made harder by internalized guilt and external judgment.

The concept of "quality time", the notion that brief periods of focused attention can substitute for quantity of presence, emerged partly as a justification for dual-career families where parents faced time scarcity. Yet research on parent-child attachment suggests the formula is more complex: children need both predictable routine presence (knowing parents will be available at certain times) and occasional extended stretches of unstructured shared time (not necessarily highly engaging, just co-present) to develop secure attachment. Quality time, intense, focused, special activities, serve essential functions but cannot fully replace simple availability. A parent who works 70 hours weekly but provides 2 hours of high-quality engagement on Saturday afternoon may satisfy specific developmental needs while leaving others unmet, particularly children's need for accessibility when they need connection rather than when it's been scheduled. The challenge becomes defining sufficient presence across multiple dimensions simultaneously: adequate routine availability, sufficient focused engagement, meaningful exceptional experiences, appropriate supervision, and sufficient absence to foster independence. Parents who successfully navigate this multidimensional sufficiency typically achieve it not through optimization but through conscious acceptance of "good enough parenting", psychologist Donald Winnicott's recognition that adequate parenting involves meeting children's essential needs reliably while accepting inevitable imperfection rather than attempting impossible perfection.

The Digital Multiplication of Relational Obligation

Social media fundamentally disrupted traditional relationship maintenance by dramatically lowering the cost of superficial interaction while simultaneously raising expectations about appropriate response rates and public acknowledgment. Before digital communication, maintaining contact with someone required either physical presence, a phone call requiring mutual availability, or written correspondence, which involved effort and postal delay. These friction points naturally limited the scope of the relationship to those worth the investment. Current technology eliminates nearly all friction: birthday notifications help you remember everyone's special day; one-click reactions let you acknowledge someone's life event without crafting a meaningful response; group messages let you maintain contact with dozens of people at once. This efficiency paradoxically creates more obligation rather than less because the lowered cost of interaction makes failure to interact more conspicuous. The person who doesn't "like" a friend's major announcement comes across as intentionally dismissive rather than simply unaware; the birthday left unacknowledged signals deliberate neglect rather than innocent forgetting.

This proliferation of micro-obligations creates what legal scholar Tim Wu calls "attention extraction", the systematic harvesting of human attention for commercial purposes through design features that maximize engagement regardless of user benefit. Every notification, prompt, and reminder represents a claim on your cognitive resources disguised as social consideration. The platform allegedly helps you maintain relationships; actually, it monetizes your attention by keeping you perpetually engaged while creating artificial relational obligations you must service to avoid social penalty. The result is that many people spend hours daily maintaining hundreds of superficial digital connections while having no energy left for substantive engagement with the people physically present in their lives. They've fulfilled numerous small relational obligations, reacting to posts, commenting on photos, responding to messages, while accomplishing zero meaningful connection. It's the relational equivalent of eating fifteen small snacks throughout the day and wondering why you feel simultaneously bloated and malnourished.

Establishing sufficiency in digital relational space requires active resistance to platform defaults and social expectations they've normalized. This might involve explicit decisions: checking social media once daily rather than continuously; disabling notifications to reclaim agency over when you attend to relational claims; unfollowing people you know in favor of following people you learn from; or periodically declaring "digital sabbaths" in which connection occurs only through high-friction channels that require genuine intention. These practices feel socially risky because they violate emerging norms about appropriate responsiveness and availability. Yet they rest on a crucial recognition: the appearance of abundant connection through frictionless digital interaction often masks genuine relational poverty. The person with sufficient intimate relationships can afford to ignore most digital relational obligations without meaningful cost to their actual social support network; the person lacking deep connections desperately services superficial digital relationships precisely because they don't have adequate offline intimacy. The remedy isn't more digital engagement but rather strategic withdrawal to protect the time, attention, and energy required for cultivating sufficient depth in a small number of relationships that actually sustain you.

Intergenerational Relationships and the Sandwich Generation Dilemma

The phenomenon demographers call the "sandwich generation", adults simultaneously caring for aging parents and dependent children, illustrates with particular force the challenge of achieving relational sufficiency when multiple constituencies make legitimate claims on limited resources. A forty-five-year-old woman managing a career, raising two teenagers, and coordinating care for her mother with advancing dementia faces mathematically impossible allocation problems. Each domain requires more attention than remains after meeting the minimum requirements in the others. Career survival demands forty-plus hours; teenagers need transportation, homework support, and emotional availability; the aging parent requires medical appointments, medication management, safety monitoring, and companionship. The numbers don't add up. Something must give, yet each obligation involves relationships with people whose needs are genuine, legitimate, and often non-negotiable.

This dilemma forces confrontation with relational triage: the explicit prioritization of some relationships over others based on urgency, dependency, and capacity for self-sufficiency. The teenager can't care for themselves; the parent can't either, but the employer expects professional performance despite these realities. Traditional solutions involved extended family networks distributing obligations across multiple adults, but geographic dispersal and smaller family sizes mean many adults face these challenges with minimal support. The question "Am I doing enough?" haunts sandwich generation adults precisely because truthful assessment reveals they cannot possibly do enough across all domains, given genuine constraints. The parent receives less attention than ideal; the children receive less presence than desired; the career receives less focus than required for advancement; one's own health and well-being get deprioritized to crisis levels. This isn't a failure of character or insufficient effort; it's a mathematical impossibility meeting social expectations designed for different demographic and economic circumstances.

Achieving something resembling sufficiency in this context requires radical acceptance of inadequacy: explicitly acknowledging you cannot meet all legitimate needs and making conscious decisions about which relationships receive what level of investment, knowing some will receive less than you wish you could provide. This might mean paid caregivers handling most parental care while you provide supervisory oversight and periodic quality time, rather than attempting hands-on caregiving that would collapse other obligations. It might mean teenagers take on household responsibilities earlier than preferred because you lack bandwidth for maintenance tasks. It might mean career advancement pauses during peak caregiving years, accepting financial costs for relational protection. None of these solutions is ideal; all involve trade-offs and losses. But they represent conscious sufficiency definitions made within real constraints rather than aspirational ideals that generate perpetual guilt about inevitable shortfalls. The adult who can articulate "I am providing enough, given actual constraints" while acknowledging limitations has achieved something more valuable than impossible perfection: realistic sufficiency that allows sustainable functioning without psychological collapse from perpetual inadequacy.

The concept of relational sufficiency ultimately requires each individual to move from implicit assumptions to explicit definition: How many intimate relationships do I need to feel adequately connected? What level of attention does each primary relationship require to remain vital? Which relationships deserve continued investment, and which have completed their natural arc? What constitutes adequate parenting, adequate partnership, adequate friendship within the actual constraints of my circumstances rather than idealized cultural fantasies? These questions lack universal answers precisely because sufficiency varies by individual temperament, life stage, and circumstantial demands. Yet avoiding these questions, hoping implicit standards will somehow produce clarity, guarantees either perpetual feelings of inadequacy or relational dilution that satisfies no one. The person who consciously defines relational sufficiency across all domains may still feel the ache of limits. Still, they escape the corrosive guilt of never knowing whether they're doing enough because they've never articulated what enough actually means.

Chapter 7: Setting Boundaries: Knowing When to Say No

The architecture of obligation in contemporary life operates through invisible yet powerful mechanisms that make refusal feel at once necessary and impossible. A colleague requests assistance with a project outside your expertise. A nonprofit organization that does admirable work solicits your volunteer time. A friend invites you to an event that conflicts with your only unscheduled evening this month. An aging parent expects weekly visits that require a 4-hour round-trip. A community board position opens that would benefit from your skills. In each instance, saying yes seems reasonable, the request is legitimate, the cause worthy, the relationship important. Yet the cumulative weight of these individual yeses creates lives of breathless over-commitment, where every obligation receives inadequate attention and the person at the center experiences perpetual guilt about disappointing everyone slightly rather than satisfying anyone fully. The difficulty lies not in recognizing that some requests must be declined but in developing functional criteria for determining which ones, and in acquiring the psychological infrastructure to decline without experiencing refusal as moral failure.

The problem intensifies because boundary-setting operates against evolutionary programming that served survival in small-group contexts. Anthropological evidence from hunter-gatherer societies suggests that reputation maintenance within stable groups of 30-150 individuals was crucial to survival. Being perceived as unhelpful or ungenerous carried existential consequences, exclusion from food-sharing networks, reduced opportunities for mate selection, and diminished collective protection during threats. This environment is selected for psychological tendencies toward compliance, particularly regarding in-group requests. Saying no to the legitimate needs of group members would have been not merely socially awkward but genuinely dangerous. The modern difficulty with boundary-setting reflects this ancestral context: our psychological machinery treats declined requests as threats to social standing and group membership, triggering anxiety responses disproportionate to actual contemporary consequences. The person who experiences elevated heart rate, racing thoughts, and persistent worry after declining to join a committee is not being irrational, they are experiencing appropriate threat responses to circumstances that no longer apply. We inhabit an environment where most requests come from loose connections rather than survival-critical group members, where reputation exists across multiple disconnected social spheres rather than one integrated community, and where saying no to one request rarely jeopardizes our position in networks that matter. Yet the alarm system continues responding as though every declined request threatens our survival.

The Consent Confusion: Obligation Versus Opportunity

A subtle but crucial distinction that undermines effective boundary-setting involves confusion between opportunities and obligations. When presented with a request, invitation, or possibility, many people unconsciously process it through an obligation framework: "Should I do this?" or "Would it be wrong to decline?" This framing turns every option into a moral test, in which refusal requires justification and acceptance serves as the default ethical position. The alternative framing treats requests as opportunities: "Do I want to do this given my current priorities and constraints?" This second approach reverses the burden; acceptance requires justification rather than refusal. The difference appears subtle but generates radically different behavioral outcomes. Research by organizational psychologist Adam Grant at the Wharton School examining prosocial behavior patterns found that individuals who frame requests as opportunities and consciously choose which to accept report significantly higher satisfaction with their helping behavior and lower burnout rates than those who frame requests as obligations. The opportunity framers help less frequently overall but experience their helping as more meaningful and sustainable. They easily decline most requests but invest deeply in the ones they accept, generating better outcomes for recipients and themselves.

The obligation framework creates what might be called "consent confusion", the inability to distinguish between things we have actively chosen and things we have passively failed to refuse. A person operating in obligation mode might serve on five committees, volunteer for three organizations, and maintain involvement in multiple community activities without genuinely wanting to participate in any of them. They consented to each commitment when asked, but that consent emerged from an inability to identify sufficient justification for refusal rather than from an authentic desire to participate. This produces a peculiar form of unfreedom: a life filled with activities the person never chose in any meaningful sense. The committee member who attends meetings while mentally composing their grocery list, the volunteer who arrives late and leaves early, the community participant who engages with visible reluctance, these are people trapped by consent confusion, unable to recognize that the absence of sufficient justification for no does not constitute adequate justification for yes. Clear boundary-setting requires reclaiming the distinction between what we have chosen and what we have merely failed to refuse, and recognizing that the latter represents a violation of personal autonomy regardless of whether the request itself was legitimate.

Some of the most consequential boundary failures occur in professional contexts where power asymmetries make refusal feel dangerous regardless of actual organizational culture. A manager who sends emails at eleven p.m. may genuinely intend no expectation of an immediate response. Still, subordinates often perceive implicit pressure to demonstrate equivalent commitment through off-hours availability. The employee who establishes a boundary, not checking email after 7 p.m., not attending optional weekend events, declining assignments beyond their role scope, risks being perceived as insufficiently dedicated even when their actual work product exceeds expectations. Research by sociologist Erin Reid at Boston University studying consultants at a prestigious firm found that employees who quietly reduced their hours while maintaining an appearance of full availability received better performance reviews than those who formally negotiated reduced schedules, despite identical work output. The finding reveals how boundary-setting often conflicts with signaling requirements: the substantive boundary (working reasonable hours) can be maintained only by violating the symbolic boundary (appearing perpetually available). This creates a psychological trap in which effective boundaries require either deception, pretending greater availability than is actually maintained, or accepting career consequences for setting reasonable limits.

The Depletion Debt: Understanding Boundary Costs

Every yes carries not just the obvious direct cost, time, and energy required for the commitment itself, but also hidden depletion costs that compound across multiple obligations. Accepting a breakfast meeting means not just the time of the meeting but also earlier wake-up, commute adjustments, energy expenditure during peak cognitive hours, and recovery time after social interaction for those who find such engagements draining. Agreeing to host a holiday gathering involves not merely the event itself but weeks of anticipatory planning, shopping expeditions, house preparation, cooking marathons, and post-event cleanup. The person who evaluates only direct costs, "It's just one hour" or "It's only one evening", systematically underestimates the actual resource drain, leading to over-commitment based on faulty accounting. Behavioral economists studying decision-making under resource constraints identify this as the "focusing illusion", the tendency to evaluate options based on their most salient feature while overlooking less obvious but equally important factors. In boundary-setting contexts, the focusing illusion makes the visible, concrete aspect of a request (the meeting, the event, the project) obscure the surrounding infrastructure of preparation, transition, recovery, and opportunity cost.

The concept of "depletion debt" helps illuminate these hidden costs. Every commitment not only consumes resources but also reduces capacity for subsequent demands. A person who accepts three social engagements in one weekend may successfully attend all three, but their Monday work performance suffers from social-energy depletion. The parent who volunteers for every school activity maintains technical presence but delivers diminished attention to their own children due to decision fatigue and attention fragmentation. Someone who sits on multiple boards may attend all meetings but contributes superficially to all rather than substantively to any. Depletion debt accumulates like financial debt, with interest: an initial over-commitment reduces capacity for careful decision-making, leading to additional poor boundary choices and accelerating the depletion spiral. Research by psychologist Roy Baumeister on ego depletion suggests that self-control is a limited resource that becomes depleted with use. Suppose boundary-setting requires self-control, resisting social pressure, tolerating discomfort, and maintaining resolve against persuasion. In that case, people who exercise boundaries frequently may paradoxically become worse at boundary maintenance over time as their self-control reservoir depletes. This creates a vulnerability window: someone who has successfully declined multiple requests may accept an unreasonable one simply because their capacity for refusal has been exhausted, much like a dieter who maintains discipline all day but raids the pantry at midnight when willpower reserves run dry.

Strategic boundary-setting, therefore, requires not just declining individual requests but also creating structural barriers that reduce the frequency of boundary-testing situations. The professional who establishes "office hours" for colleague requests rather than maintaining perpetual accessibility minimizes the number of decisions required. The parent who institutes a standing family rule, "We don't schedule activities on Sunday", eliminates the need for repeated negotiations about weekend commitments. The friend who sets a monthly rhythm, "I can get together on the second Saturday of each month", provides connection while preventing schedule fragmentation. These structural boundaries function as decision-making infrastructure, removing multiple small choices that would each require self-control expenditure. Behavioral scientist Wendy Wood's research on habit formation shows that approximately 43% of daily behaviors occur at the exact location and roughly the same time, suggesting that much of life operates on autopilot rather than through active choice. People with sustainable boundaries leverage this automaticity by creating default structures that don't require repeated conscious refusal. The person who must actively decline each request depletes their boundary-maintenance capacity; the person who has established structural defaults that handle most requests automatically preserves their decision-making resources for genuinely ambiguous situations that warrant careful consideration.

The Guilt Asymmetry and Reciprocity Myths

One of the most psychologically burdensome aspects of boundary-setting involves what might be termed "guilt asymmetry", the phenomenon in which declining a request generates internal guilt, while accepting an unwanted commitment primarily generates external burden. When someone asks us to help them move, declining produces immediate guilt: we imagine their disappointment, wonder whether we're being selfish, and worry about damaging the relationship. Accepting the request transfers the cost from emotional (guilt) to practical (time, physical effort, schedule disruption), and sensible costs feel more acceptable than emotional ones, even when they're objectively larger. This asymmetry makes boundary violations feel like the path of least resistance: saying yes hurts others while saying no hurts ourselves. Hence, those socialized toward other-orientation habitually choose the option that preserves external harmony at the expense of internal resources. The problem compounds because guilt is immediate while depletion accumulates gradually. The person who accepts too many commitments experiences a slow-building overwhelm, while the person who declines a request experiences instant guilt. The temporal asymmetry makes boundary violations attractive in the moment, even though their cumulative effect proves more damaging than acute guilt would have been.

This dynamic intensifies through what psychologists call the "reciprocity principle", the deeply ingrained expectation that helping others creates social credit we can later redeem when we need assistance. Evolutionary psychologist Robert Trivers' research on reciprocal altruism suggests this principle supported survival in ancestral environments where individuals regularly needed help beyond their immediate capabilities and could access it only through networks of mutual obligation. Someone who helped retrieve a neighbor's escaped livestock could expect reciprocal assistance when their own livestock wandered, creating an insurance system against individual misfortune. In such contexts, declining to help when capable would rationally reduce others' willingness to assist you in the future. Contemporary life operates according to a fundamentally different logic that undermines reciprocity as a boundary-setting guide. Most requests come from relationships that lack genuine reciprocity potential. The charity solicitor will never help you move, the distant acquaintance requesting professional advice has no resources you need, and the organization seeking volunteers cannot volunteer for you. Even in relationships with theoretical reciprocity potential, modern specialized existence means people rarely need the specific forms of help others can provide. The colleague whose computer expertise you assist may never need the marketing advice you could offer. The friend you help with childcare may have no elderly parents when you eventually need elder care support.

More fundamentally, reciprocity as a boundary criterion creates a transactional framework that corrodes the intrinsic satisfaction of genuine helping. Research by motivation psychologist Edward Deci distinguishes between autonomous helping, assistance freely chosen based on an authentic desire to contribute, and controlled helping, assistance provided under external pressure, obligation, or the expectation of a future return. Autonomous helping correlates with increased well-being for the helper, while controlled helping associates with resentment and burnout. When people maintain inadequate boundaries due to reciprocity concerns, they transform potentially meaningful helping into controlled obligation, simultaneously reducing their satisfaction and often providing lower-quality assistance. The person who agrees to help but resents the imposition delivers begrudging, minimal effort that may technically fulfill the commitment while violating its spirit. Both parties would have benefited if the boundary had been maintained: the requester could have found an actually willing helper, and the reluctant helper could have preserved resources for opportunities they actually wanted to pursue. Yet the reciprocity myth keeps people trapped in cycles of joyless obligation, accumulating social debts that cannot be redeemed as they imagine, while depleting their capacity for autonomous helping that would genuinely nourish both themselves and their communities.

The Priority Clarity Prerequisite

The most effective boundary-setters share a characteristic that makes their refusals straightforward: they possess unusual clarity about their priorities. When someone with clear priorities receives a request, they evaluate it against an explicit hierarchy of commitments and values. If it aligns with high priorities and they have adequate capacity, they accept; if not, they decline without extensive anguish. The person lacking priority clarity faces a fundamentally different task: every request requires constructing an ad-hoc decision framework, comparing incommensurable goods, and hoping their choice proves correct. This difference explains why boundary-setting advice, "Just say no" or "Put yourself first", proves useless for most people. The person struggling with boundaries doesn't need permission to decline or encouragement toward self-interest; they need the foundational clarity that would make decisions obvious. Telling someone without a priority hierarchy to "just say no" is like instructing someone without a map to "just navigate"; the problem isn't a lack of willingness but the absence of the prerequisites that make the task straightforward.

Developing clarity about priorities requires confronting questions most people avoid: What matters enough to justify significant resource allocation? What activities or relationships deserve protection even when competing demands emerge? What would I need to abandon to make space for what I claim to value most? These questions are uncomfortable because they force us to recognize our finitude; we cannot pursue every worthy goal, maintain every valuable relationship, or explore every interesting opportunity. Priority clarity means accepting that saying yes to some things requires saying no to other things that also have merit. The parent who prioritizes being present for their children's evening routine must decline professional networking dinners, accepting that career advancement will be slower. The artist who protects morning hours for creative work must refuse social engagements the night before, accepting reduced social connection. The activist who commits deeply to one cause must ignore other equally deserving issues, accepting that their contribution to justice will be narrower than their concern. This acceptance, that our choices inevitably disappoint someone, sometimes ourselves, represents the psychological work that precedes effective boundary-setting.

Some individuals discover clarity about priorities through crisis, a health emergency that reveals what actually matters. This relationship rupture clarifies whose presence is essential, a professional failure that exposes which achievements they genuinely value versus which they pursued for external validation. These crucible experiences provide involuntary priority clarification by removing options and forcing choices that reveal underlying values. The person recovering from burnout may realize they sacrificed well-being for career advancement they didn't actually want; the individual whose friend group contracts after establishing boundaries learns which relationships had genuine substance versus which depended on unconditional availability. However, waiting for a crisis to provide clarity on priorities proves unnecessarily costly. More proactive approaches involve structured reflection: journaling exercises that explore tensions between stated values and actual time allocation, discussions with trusted others who can provide an external perspective on patterns we're too embedded to see, and experimental boundary-setting in low-stakes domains to test which refusals generate relief versus regret. The goal is developing what philosopher Harry Frankfurt calls "volitional necessity", the experience of recognizing that specific commitments are so essential to our identity that violating them feels like self-betrayal. When a request conflicts with volitional necessity, declining becomes straightforward because acceptance would require abandoning something we're psychologically unable to sacrifice. The parent who experiences volitional necessity around bedtime presence doesn't agonize about whether to accept an evening work commitment; the answer is automatic because the alternative is unthinkable.

The transformation from ambiguous priority struggle to clear priority hierarchy doesn't eliminate difficult choices, but it converts them from identity crises into practical logistics. The person with clear priorities still receives requests that conflict with their commitments, still experiences pressure to accommodate others, and still faces social consequences for maintaining boundaries. The difference lies in decisional confidence: they know which commitments deserve protection, which relationships warrant investment, and which opportunities align with their actual path. Their no's emerge from clarity rather than self-doubt, making them simultaneously easier to deliver and more resistant to external pressure. When someone asks why you can't help and you genuinely don't know which priority would justify refusal, negotiation begins. When you know precisely which commitment makes acceptance impossible, the boundary becomes non-negotiable. The former invites persuasion and guilt; the latter states reality. The hard work of boundary-setting isn't learning to say no, it's developing the clarity of priorities that makes the no self-evident.

Chapter 8: The Role of Gratitude in Finding Enough

The practice of gratitude occupies a peculiar position in contemporary discourse, simultaneously ubiquitous and profoundly misunderstood. Corporate wellness programs encourage employees to maintain gratitude journals. Self-help influencers prescribe daily gratitude lists as cure-alls for dissatisfaction. Motivational posters command us to "be grateful" with the same insistence once reserved for "work harder" or "think positively." Yet this popularization has hollowed out gratitude's radical core, transforming a sophisticated cognitive practice into a compliance mechanism that asks us to feel thankful for inadequate circumstances rather than address them. The gratitude-industrial complex peddles a version of appreciation that functions as an anesthetic rather than awakening, a tool for manufacturing contentment with insufficient wages, exploitative relationships, and systemic inequities by directing attention toward whatever meager satisfactions remain available. This corruption obscures gratitude's genuine relationship to sufficiency, which operates through mechanisms entirely different from the superficial thankfulness these programs promote. Authentic gratitude does not ask us to be satisfied with less than enough; rather, it recalibrates our perceptual apparatus to recognize when enough has actually been achieved, cutting through the manufactured scarcity that prevents us from experiencing adequacy even when it surrounds us. Understanding this distinction requires excavating gratitude from the self-help rubble and examining how it actually functions as a cognitive technology for perceiving sufficiency.

The neurological mechanics of gratitude reveal why it serves as such a powerful instrument for recognizing enough. When we engage in authentic grateful attention, not performative listing but genuine acknowledgment of value received, we activate what neuroscientist Alex Korb identifies as the brain's reward and motivation circuits in ways that fundamentally differ from both pleasure and achievement. Gratitude stimulates the anterior cingulate cortex and medial prefrontal cortex, regions involved in moral cognition, value judgment, and perspective-taking. Simultaneously, it modulates amygdala activity, reducing threat sensitivity and the anxiety that drives acquisitive behavior. This neural pattern creates what cognitive scientists call "present-moment anchoring", a state in which attention fixes on what exists now rather than on what might exist in imagined futures or alternative presents. This anchoring is critical because the inability to recognize sufficiency stems largely from temporal displacement: we evaluate our present circumstances against fantasized futures in which different choices would have yielded superior outcomes, or against curated presentations of others' lives that bear little resemblance to lived reality. By neurologically binding attention to present circumstances and their actual value rather than their comparative position in imagined hierarchies, gratitude creates the cognitive conditions under which "enough" becomes perceptible rather than perpetually deferred.

Research by psychologists Robert Emmons and Michael McCullough, conducted through controlled longitudinal studies, provides empirical evidence for gratitude's role in perceiving sufficiency. However, the mechanisms they documented differ significantly from popular assumptions. Participants who maintained weekly gratitude journals for ten weeks, noting five things for which they felt grateful, reported higher life satisfaction and optimism compared to control groups who recorded either hassles or neutral events. More significantly, the gratitude group exhibited decreased materialism scores and reduced desire for consumption across multiple product categories. This finding is counterintuitive: why would noting positive aspects of life decrease desire for additional positive experiences? The answer lies in what Emmons terms "the amplification effect." Gratitude practice doesn't create satisfaction with deprivation but rather amplifies awareness of value already present. A person who never consciously attends to their friendships might feel lonely despite having several genuine connections; attention fragmented across dozens of shallow relationships prevents depth perception. Grateful attention to existing friendships doesn't manufacture friendship where none exists, but makes existing relational wealth perceptible and experientially tangible. The decrease in materialism reflects not resignation but recognition; participants needed to acquire less because they could finally perceive what they already possessed.

Gratitude as Pattern Interruption

The relentless habituation that prevents us from experiencing adequacy operates through what psychologists call the "hedonic treadmill," but this metaphor misleads by suggesting continuous motion. More accurately, habituation functions as perceptual fading: repeated exposure to a stimulus gradually causes it to disappear from conscious awareness. You notice the humming refrigerator only when it stops. You feel your clothing only when first putting it on, then tactile awareness vanishes. This fading serves essential evolutionary functions; attending to unchanging stimuli wastes cognitive resources better allocated to detecting novelty and threat. However, applied to life circumstances, habituation creates the paradox of invisible adequacy: the functional home, the reliable health, the available food, the present relationships all fade from awareness precisely because they consistently deliver what we need. We notice the water only when the well runs dry; gratitude functions as a deliberate pattern interruption that forces perceptual refresh. By consciously directing attention to what habituation has rendered invisible, grateful acknowledgment makes the adequate experientially available once again. This process differs fundamentally from "counting blessings," which implies evaluating quantity. Gratitude practice involves qualitative re-perception: making familiar things strange again so that their actual value registers consciously.

Anthropological research on gift economies illuminates gratitude's role in establishing perceptions of sufficiency through social rather than individual mechanisms. In societies organized around reciprocal gift-giving rather than market exchange, studied extensively by anthropologist David Graeber in Madagascar and other non-monetized communities, gratitude functions not as individual sentiment but as a social technology for creating balanced flows. When someone receives a gift, the gratitude expressed simultaneously acknowledges receipt, validates the relationship, and establishes future reciprocity obligation. This transaction doesn't calculate exact equivalence; instead, it creates an ongoing connection through continuous flow. Nobody tracks whether they've received exactly as much as they've given; instead, the community maintains awareness of general balance over time. This system reveals a crucial aspect of sufficiency: it emerges from dynamics rather than static accumulation. The person is sufficient not because they possess adequate stockpiles but because they're embedded in networks of reliable flow. Translating this to individual practice, gratitude reconceptualizes sufficiency from "having enough things" to "having enough flow", enough nutrition coming in, enough creativity going out, enough learning arriving, enough contribution departing. This shift from stock to flow thinking fundamentally alters what "enough" means and makes it much more achievable because flow can be sufficient even when stocks remain modest.

The practice of what contemplative traditions call "discriminating gratitude" offers a sophisticated tool for distinguishing genuine sufficiency from manufactured inadequacy. This approach doesn't ask us to feel grateful for everything indiscriminately, a request that borders on gaslighting when applied to genuinely harmful circumstances. Instead, it involves conscious discernment about what genuinely serves our wellbeing versus what undermines it. A person might feel genuine gratitude for employment that provides a stable income while simultaneously recognizing that the workplace culture harms their health; gratitude for financial security doesn't require manufactured expressions of thankfulness for exploitation. This discrimination matters because it prevents gratitude from functioning as passivity. Research by organizational psychologist Amy Wrzesniewski at Yale, studying workers across multiple industries, found that individuals who practiced discriminating gratitude, appreciating specific positive aspects while clearly acknowledging deficiencies, maintained higher motivation for improvement than those who practiced either indiscriminate gratitude or an exclusive focus on problems. The discriminating group could recognize when their situation contained elements of sufficiency worth protecting while simultaneously identifying aspects requiring change. They didn't feel compelled to choose between appreciation and advocacy, gratitude and boundaries. This capacity to hold both perspectives simultaneously creates the psychological ground for actually achieving sufficiency rather than simply resigning ourselves to inadequacy.

Gratitude Literacy and Emotional Granularity

The poverty of English's vocabulary of gratitude constrains our capacity to use appreciation as a tool for recognizing different forms of sufficiency. We collapse distinct experiences, relief, appreciation, wonder, recognition, satisfaction, and indebtedness under the single term "gratitude," losing crucial distinctions in the process. Psychologist Lisa Feldman Barrett's research on emotional granularity shows that individuals with richer emotion vocabularies, who can distinguish subtle variations in emotional experience, show better emotional regulation and greater psychological resilience. The same principle applies to gratitude. Relief at avoiding harm differs fundamentally from appreciation for unexpected beauty, yet both might get classified simply as "feeling grateful." This linguistic compression matters because different forms of gratitude point toward other aspects of sufficiency. Relief indicates we've met a baseline need; appreciation suggests we've exceeded necessity into genuine flourishing; wonder signals encounters with value beyond our capacity to possess or control. Developing gratitude literacy, learning to distinguish these variations, creates a more sophisticated instrument for calibrating sufficiency. Instead of a binary "grateful/ungrateful," we develop a spectrum of responses that provide detailed feedback about which needs are met, which remain unaddressed, and which have been exceeded into genuine abundance.

The temporal dimension of gratitude proves particularly crucial for establishing sufficiency. Modern psychology typically treats gratitude as focused on the present or recent past, appreciating what we have now or what we recently received. However, indigenous gratitude practices studied by ethnographer Enrique Salmón among Rarámuri communities in Mexico reveal more complex temporal orientations. Their gratitude practices extend backward across generations, acknowledging ancestors who created current possibilities, and forward toward descendants who will inherit the consequences of present choices. This expanded temporal frame transforms gratitude from individual sentiment into intergenerational positioning. When considering a purchase, the question becomes not just "Am I grateful for what I already have?" but "How will my descendants regard my choices? Will they feel I stewarded resources toward genuine flourishing or squandered them on ephemeral satisfaction?" This ancestral-descendant framework makes sufficiency a relational determination rather than an individual calculation. Enough becomes not "enough for me now" but "enough for us across time", a radically different standard that both elevates the threshold in some domains (requiring greater attention to sustainability and legacy) while lowering it in others (reducing pressure for personal aggrandizement that serves no one beyond ourselves).

Research by positive psychologists Philip Watkins and Tamara Scheibe investigating the relationship between gratitude and desire demonstrates a paradoxical finding: individuals who score highest on gratitude measures don't experience less desire than others, but rather experience desire differently. High-gratitude individuals report equivalent wanting but dramatically less suffering when wants remain unsatisfied. This distinction reveals gratitude's actual function with respect to sufficiency. It doesn't eliminate desire, a goal both impossible and undesirable since desire drives growth, creativity, and improvement. Rather, gratitude decouples desire from desperation. We can want things while simultaneously recognizing that not obtaining them won't fundamentally threaten our wellbeing because we're already embedded in sufficiency. This psychological position, what the researchers term "grounded wanting", allows us to pursue improvement and expansion without the anxiety that drives compulsive acquisition. The person can desire a better job while genuinely appreciating the current one, explore new relationships while valuing existing connections, and pursue learning while acknowledging present competence. This grounded desire dramatically reduces the psychological suffering that comes from gap-focused consciousness, the perpetual measuring of the distance between the current state and the desired state that makes the present feel like inadequacy regardless of objective circumstances.

The practice of "gratitude witnessing", verbally expressing appreciation to others for specific actions or qualities, serves functions that private gratitude journaling cannot replicate. When we tell someone specifically what we appreciate about them or what they did that benefited us, we accomplish several things simultaneously. We make our perception of value explicit and public, reducing the likelihood that habituation will erase it again. We strengthen the relationship by demonstrating that we notice and value the other person's contributions, typically increasing their future investment. We model grateful attention for witnesses to the exchange, potentially spreading the practice through social learning. Most critically for sufficiency perception, we discover that articulation demands specificity; generic statements ring hollow, forcing us to identify particular moments and qualities. This enforced precision rebuilds perceptual acuity that habituation degrades. A marriage counselor described a couple in crisis whose relationship transformed when they committed to expressing one specific act of gratitude to each other every day. Initially, both struggled to find anything beyond generic appreciation. Within three weeks, each partner noticed multiple specific moments worthy of acknowledgment, not because the other's behavior improved, but because the practice rebuilt perception. They'd lived amid relational adequacy; they literally couldn't see until grateful attention forced them to look more carefully. The relationship hadn't become sufficient; they'd learned to perceive the sufficiency that surrounded them.

Gratitude's relationship to sufficiency ultimately reveals something unexpected: adequacy is not primarily a material condition but a perceptual capacity. Two individuals with identical resources experience radically different levels of sufficiency based on their ability to recognize value in what they possess. This reality doesn't justify deprivation or excuse inequality, genuine poverty exists and causes real suffering that gratitude cannot remedy. However, in the vast middle territory where basic needs are met but satisfaction remains elusive, gratitude functions as the cognitive technology that makes the transition from objective adequacy to experienced sufficiency. It serves as the bridge between having enough and recognizing that we have enough, closing the gap that consumer culture works tirelessly to maintain. This bridging function explains why gratitude proves so threatening to economic systems requiring perpetual consumption growth: populations skilled at perceiving sufficiency represent demand failures, people who've stopped running on the acquisition treadmill not through deprivation but through perceptual transformation. The person who can see abundance in modest circumstances possesses a form of wealth that no economy can capture or tax, a prosperity that exists independent of market participation. This capacity, to experience enough as enough, represents not resignation to limitation but mastery of the perceptual art that determines whether our material circumstances translate into genuine flourishing or remain perpetually inadequate despite their objective abundance.

The Gratitude-Comparison Paradox

Contemporary gratitude practice confronts a peculiar contradiction that reveals much about the cultural construction of sufficiency. Psychology research consistently demonstrates that social comparison, measuring ourselves against others, undermines well-being and generates feelings of inadequacy. Yet one of the most common gratitude prompts instructs practitioners to "think of those less fortunate than yourself." This comparative gratitude, feeling thankful because others have less, contains troubling implications. It positions our sufficiency as dependent on others' deprivation, creates what philosopher Sara Ahmed calls "happiness duty," where we're obligated to feel satisfied because someone somewhere suffers more, and fundamentally misunderstands how sufficiency operates. Psychologist Jordi Quoidbach's research at the University of Barcelona examined whether comparative gratitude (appreciating what you have by contrasting it with what others have less) produced different outcomes than intrinsic gratitude (appreciating what you have based on its inherent value to you). The findings proved striking: participants induced to practice comparative gratitude showed temporary mood elevation but increased anxiety about loss and heightened sensitivity to social status. Those practicing intrinsic gratitude demonstrated sustained improvements in well-being and decreased concern with relative position. The mechanism appears to be that comparative gratitude still operates within scarcity consciousness; your adequacy depends on winning a zero-sum comparison. Intrinsic gratitude escapes this framework entirely by recognizing value that exists independent of distribution, possession that isn't diminished by others also possessing it. When I appreciate my friend's kindness, the fact that you also have kind friends doesn't reduce my sufficiency. When I feel grateful for a comparative advantage, I have more than you; my sufficiency becomes unstable, dependent on maintaining a hierarchical position.

This distinction proves crucial for cultivating gratitude that genuinely supports a sense of sufficiency rather than merely manufacturing temporary contentment with hierarchical position. Clinical psychologist Sonja Lyubomirsky's interventional studies at UC Riverside found that gratitude practices structured around "What brought value to your life this week?" produced significantly more durable increases in life satisfaction than those structured around "What do you have that others lack?" The difference in framing shifted gratitude from a positional good to an intrinsic good, from a relative advantage to an absolute value. Participants in the intrinsic-value condition maintained elevated well-being scores for six months post-intervention; those in the comparative condition returned to baseline within weeks. The research suggests that sustainable sufficiency perception requires anchoring adequacy in qualities that don't depend on scarcity or competitive advantage, experiences like learning, connection, creativity, beauty, growth, domains where others' participation enhances rather than threatens your sufficiency. A thousand people hearing the same music doesn't reduce your experience of it; a thousand people loving deeply doesn't deplete the available love. Gratitude for these non-rivalrous goods cultivates sufficiency that can be genuinely shared rather than possessed at others' expense.

Prospective Gratitude and Future Sufficiency

While most gratitude research focuses on appreciation for past or present goods, emerging work on "prospective gratitude", appreciation for future possibilities, reveals another dimension of sufficiency perception. Psychologist Glenn Fox at USC's Brain and Creativity Institute discovered through fMRI studies that imagining future scenarios and feeling grateful for possibilities not yet realized activate both the brain's reward prediction circuits and its empathy networks simultaneously. This combined activation creates what Fox terms "possibility awareness", the recognition that adequate futures are within reach, that sufficiency tomorrow doesn't require lottery winnings or radical transformation but rather the continuation and modest development of present trajectories. This prospective orientation counters the anxiety that views every current adequacy as precarious, every sufficiency as temporary. The person who can feel grateful for tomorrow's possibilities, not with magical thinking that ignores real threats but with grounded recognition of reasonably expectable continuity, experiences their present sufficiency as more stable. They don't frantically over-accumulate as a hedge against imagined catastrophe because they can perceive that adequate futures grow organically from adequate presents. This temporal extension of gratitude creates a sufficiency that spans time rather than existing only in vulnerable moments, laying the psychological groundwork for recognizing enough as a condition rather than a fleeting state.

Chapter 9: Balancing Ambition with Contentment

The tension between ambition and contentment represents one of the most misunderstood dialectics in human psychology. Conventional wisdom presents these forces as opposites locked in zero-sum competition, and pursuing goals requires discontentment with present circumstances, while accepting current conditions means abandoning aspirations for improvement. This framing creates an impossible choice: remain perpetually dissatisfied while striving, or achieve peace by relinquishing dreams. Yet this binary collapses under scrutiny. The most accomplished individuals across domains, from Olympic athletes to scientific researchers to master craftspeople, frequently report simultaneous states that outside observers perceive as contradictory: complete acceptance of their current capabilities alongside relentless pursuit of improvement. The mountaineer Alex Honnold, who free-soloed El Capitan without safety equipment in a feat requiring absolute present-moment focus, describes his mental state during preparation not as dissatisfaction with his skills but as curiosity about their boundaries. The cellist Yo-Yo Ma speaks of feeling complete gratitude for his current musical understanding while remaining fascinated by unexplored technical possibilities. These individuals have discovered something crucial: ambition and contentment operate on different axes rather than opposite ends of a single spectrum. Contentment addresses sufficiency, the question "Is who I am right now acceptable?" Ambition addresses direction of becoming, the question "What might I explore or develop next?" The conflict emerges only when we confuse these axes, treating ambition as evidence of insufficient being, or contentment as resignation from becoming.

Understanding this distinction requires examining what psychologists call "achievement motivation architecture", the underlying psychological structures that drive goal pursuit. Research by Carol Dweck at Stanford University distinguishes between "performance goals" focused on demonstrating competence to others, and "mastery goals" focused on developing competence for its own sake. Individuals oriented toward performance goals experience goal pursuit as anxiety-inducing: each challenge threatens to expose inadequacy, and achievement delivers only temporary relief before the next test of worth. This orientation creates genuine incompatibility between ambition and contentment because the former requires maintaining a perpetual deficit narrative, "I am not yet good enough", that precludes present acceptance. Mastery-oriented individuals experience goal pursuit very differently: challenges are seen as opportunities for learning rather than judgment, and skill development itself provides intrinsic satisfaction independent of external validation. This orientation enables what developmental psychologist Robert Kegan calls "self-transforming mind", the capacity to pursue development without treating the current self as deficient. The mastery-oriented athlete training for Olympic competition feels no contradiction between complete acceptance of current performance and dedicated pursuit of improvement because the quest itself expresses wholeness rather than compensating for inadequacy. The shift from performance to mastery orientation transforms ambition from evidence of insufficiency into expression of sufficiency, from "I must improve because I am not enough" to "I may develop further because I am secure enough to risk growth."

The Paradox of Aspirational Identity

Contemporary culture encourages the construction of what sociologist Erving Goffman termed "aspirational identity", defining ourselves not by who we are but by who we intend to become. The person who has run twice introduces themselves as "a runner." The individual who wrote three chapters calls themselves "a novelist." This aspirational framing appears motivating: claiming the identity creates commitment to behaviors that actualize it. However, aspirational identity creates severe psychological problems by fracturing present experience into "real self" and "ideal self" in ways that render current existence perpetually provisional. The aspirational runner experiences actual runs not as complete activities but as steps toward an imagined future in which they will "truly" be a runner, perhaps after completing a marathon, achieving a specific pace, or running for a certain number of consecutive years. This deferral of identity legitimacy creates what philosopher Charles Taylor calls "horizon sickness", the condition of living perpetually toward a receding future that never arrives as present reality. Each achievement moves the threshold: complete the marathon and discover that "real" runners qualify for Boston; achieve that and learn that "serious" runners compete in ultramarathons. The provisional nature of aspirational identity makes present accomplishment psychologically unavailable as satisfaction, regardless of objective achievement level.

The alternative involves what Zen practitioners call "identity immediacy", defining ourselves through present engagement rather than future attainment. The identity-immediate runner IS a runner because they ran this morning, not because they will complete some future goal. This framing might seem to diminish ambition by removing incentive. If we already ARE what we aspire toward, why pursue development? Yet the opposite occurs. Identity immediacy removes the achievement threshold that must be crossed before legitimacy arrives, allowing engagement with the activity itself rather than the symbolic validation it represents. Research by psychologist Kennon Sheldon examining autonomous versus controlled motivation demonstrates that individuals who engage in activities for intrinsic reasons (enjoyment, curiosity, value alignment) persist significantly longer and perform substantially better than those motivated by external validation (proving worth, gaining status, meeting others' expectations). Identity immediacy enables intrinsic engagement by eliminating the gap between the current self and the legitimate self that characterizes aspirational identity. Paradoxically, accepting "I am a runner now" fosters more sustainable development than "I will become a runner eventually," because the former draws on satisfaction to generate motivation. At the same time, the latter relies on deprivation to manufacture it. The person who runs because they enjoy being a runner develops differently from the person who runs to become a runner; the first explores the identity playfully. In contrast, the second pursues credentials grimly to gain entry to it.

This principle extends beyond individual activities to entire life trajectories. Career counseling typically encourages aspirational framing: "Where do you want to be in five years? What position are you working toward?" These questions implicitly devalue the present position as a stepping stone rather than a legitimate occupation. The assistant professor views their current role as a temporary inconvenience endured until achieving the "real" position of tenured faculty; the junior analyst tolerates their job while waiting to become senior management. This perpetual deferral creates what organizational psychologist Amy Wrzesniewski calls "job versus calling orientation." Individuals with a job orientation view work instrumentally, as a means to income or a future position, and report low engagement and satisfaction regardless of the objective role quality. Those with a calling orientation view their current work as a meaningful contribution irrespective of title or rank, and report high engagement even in objectively challenging conditions. Crucially, calling orientation correlates more strongly with subjective framing than with objective job characteristics: nurses, teachers, and administrative assistants demonstrate a complete range from job to calling orientation, suggesting that meaning derives from an interpretive stance rather than from inherent role properties. The person who treats their current position as sufficient while remaining open to development navigates work fundamentally differently than one who treats their current role as insufficient pending future advancement.

Temporal Architecture and Development Windows

The standard model of personal development encourages the simultaneous pursuit of improvements across multiple domains: advancing your career while improving your fitness, learning new skills, deepening relationships, and pursuing creative projects. This additive approach assumes that ambition across domains reinforces rather than competes, and that comprehensive self-optimization represents the highest form of human flourishing. However, research by psychologist Anders Ericsson on deliberate practice reveals that exceptional skill development requires sustained, focused attention to specific domains, which necessarily preclude simultaneous advancement across multiple areas. Ericsson's studies of expert performers across fields, musicians, athletes, chess players, and surgeons, consistently show that elite achievement requires approximately ten thousand hours of effortful practice targeting specific skill components. This investment cannot be distributed across domains without proportionally reducing advancement in each. The person attempting to simultaneously develop professional expertise, become a serious marathoner, master a musical instrument, and maintain intensive relationships will achieve mediocrity across all domains rather than excellence in any. This creates what developmental psychologist Daniel Levinson identified as "life structure conflict", the incompatibility between breadth of engagement and depth of achievement.

Resolving this conflict requires what I term "temporal architecture", consciously sequencing developmental ambitions across life stages rather than pursuing them simultaneously. The medical resident accepts that their twenties will prioritize professional competence development while relationships and other pursuits receive maintenance-level attention; the new parent recognizes that early childhood years involve intensive family engagement while career advancement temporarily plateaus; the mid-career professional might dedicate evenings to creative skill development that work demands previously prevented. This sequential approach contradicts cultural messaging about "having it all" or maintaining "work-life balance" (a misleading term that suggests equal, simultaneous investment across domains). However, sequential architecture enables actual depth that simultaneous pursuit prevents. Research by organizational scholar Jeffrey Pfeffer examining work intensity patterns found that professionals who accepted concentrated work periods followed by genuine recovery phases maintained higher performance and reported greater satisfaction than those attempting to sustain consistent moderate engagement indefinitely. The principle extends to developmental ambitions: concentrated focus on specific capabilities during appropriate windows, followed by maintenance while other capabilities receive development focus, generates superior outcomes across the lifespan compared to dispersed, continuous partial attention across all domains.

This approach requires discernment about what psychologist Mihaly Csikszentmihalyi calls "complexity", the combination of differentiation and integration. Complexity increases when we develop distinct capabilities that we can subsequently integrate into unified functionality. Learning a foreign language, growing technical expertise, cultivating artistic skill, and building relationship capacities represent differentiating developments; applying these capabilities synergistically in work or life represents integration. The error involves pursuing differentiation without integration windows, accumulating capabilities without synthesizing them into a coherent function. The person who learns conversational Spanish, completes a coding bootcamp, takes watercolor classes, and attends communication workshops has acquired skills but not necessarily increased complexity unless these skills integrate into an integrated capability. Temporal architecture should therefore alternate between differentiation phases, developing new distinct skills, and integration phases, synthesizing existing capabilities into unified competence. The professional who spends three years intensively developing technical skills, then two years learning leadership capabilities, then several years integrating both into effective team management, demonstrates greater complexity development than one attempting to simultaneously grow all dimensions continuously.

The Ambition Calibration Problem

Perhaps the most subtle challenge in balancing ambition with contentment involves what engineers would call "calibration", ensuring that ambition magnitude aligns with available resources and psychological capacity. Ambition can be insufficiently calibrated in two directions: undershooting available capacity creates stagnation and unrealized potential; overshooting creates perpetual failure and demoralization. Contemporary culture primarily warns against undercalibration, playing small, avoiding risk, and settling for comfort over growth. However, systematic overcalibration may represent the more prevalent contemporary problem, particularly among educated professionals experiencing what organizational psychologists term "optimization culture", the expectation that we should continuously maximize performance across all life domains. Research by psychologists Barry Schwartz and Andrew Ward on "maximizing versus satisficing" decision styles reveals that individuals who consistently seek optimal outcomes rather than satisfactory ones report significantly lower well-being, greater regret, and more depression despite achieving objectively superior results. This pattern suggests that the magnitude of ambition, independent of achievement, affects psychological well-being. The person pursuing optimal outcomes in career, relationships, health, personal development, and leisure will achieve more across domains than one satisfied with "good enough," but will experience that achievement as less satisfying precisely because the standard for sufficiency remains perpetually unmet.

Proper calibration requires assessing three factors rarely examined consciously: resource availability (time, energy, money, attention), recovery capacity (how much depletion you can absorb before effectiveness declines), and intrinsic motivation intensity (how much the pursuit itself satisfies independent of outcomes). Ambitions that require resources you lack, exceed the recovery capacity you possess, or pursue outcomes you don't intrinsically value create systematic failure regardless of effort quality. The person with young children, aging parents, and intensive work demands who launches a startup, trains for an Ironman triathlon, and commits to writing a novel has miscalibrated ambition against available resources: something will necessarily receive inadequate attention, leading to cascading failures across domains. Similarly, ambitions exceeding recovery capacity, the ability to sustain high-intensity effort, absorb setbacks, and maintain motivation amid difficulty, can lead to burnout regardless of initial commitment. Athletes understand periodization, alternating high-intensity training with recovery, because physical capacity development requires both stress and restoration. Ambition calibration requires psychological periodization: intensity cycles that respect recovery requirements rather than maintaining constant maximum effort. Research by organizational scholar Erin Reid found that professionals who took genuine vacation breaks maintained higher annual productivity than those working consistently, suggesting that strategic ambition reduction paradoxically enables greater long-term achievement than relentless pursuit.

Integration: The Sufficiency of Striving

The resolution of tension between ambition and contentment emerges not from choosing between them but from recognizing their complementary functions. Contentment addresses the question "Is my current existence acceptable?" while ambition addresses "What developments interest me?" These questions operate on different registers: the first concerns being, the second becoming. Problems arise only when we treat ambition as evidence of discontent or contentment as a prohibition of ambition. The master craftsperson embodies this integration: complete satisfaction with their current skill level coexists with persistent curiosity about unexplored techniques. They don't pursue mastery because current competence is inadequate, but because the pursuit itself represents a satisfying form of engagement. This orientation transforms

113

development from compensatory behavior, fixing deficiency, into expressive behavior, manifesting sufficiency. The difference is subtle but psychologically profound: compensatory development never achieves completion because each improvement reveals new deficiencies. In contrast, expressive development continues to satisfy because the activity itself fulfills rather than works toward future fulfillment.

Philosopher John Dewey distinguished between "ends-in-view" and "end-states" in ways that illuminate this integration. End-states represent final destinations where activity ceases: the completed manuscript, the achieved rank, the accumulated wealth. Ends-in-view represent directions of movement that organize present activity without requiring completion, the orientation toward clearer writing, more profound expertise, or financial security. End-states generate compensatory motivation: we work to finish so we can stop. Ends-in-view generate expressive motivation: we work because the direction itself engages us. The writer pursuing the end-state of "published novel" experiences writing as an obstacle between the current state and desired destination; the writer oriented toward clearer expression experiences writing as the activity itself, with publication as a natural consequence rather than a validating goal. This distinction explains why many people experience post-achievement depression: reaching end-states eliminates the organizing purpose that structured daily activity, creating a vacuum rather than satisfaction. Ends-in-view avoid this collapse because they persist independent of specific achievements; the pursuit of clearer expression continues regardless of publication status.

Practically implementing this integration requires regular evaluation of what psychologist Shalom Schwartz calls "value-behavior alignment", the degree to which our actual activities express our considered priorities rather than unconscious reactivity or external pressure. Most people discover significant misalignment when examining actual time allocation against stated values: they claim relationships matter most but spend minimal undistracted time with partners; they value health yet allocate no time for exercise or cooking; they treasure learning but consume only passive entertainment. This misalignment doesn't reflect hypocrisy but rather the absence of deliberate architecture: without conscious design, urgent demands displace essential commitments, and ambition is channeled toward domains that provide immediate feedback rather than deep satisfaction. Creating alignment requires what organizational theorists call "strategic abandonment", consciously identifying pursuits that no longer serve development and actively discontinuing them to protect resources for priorities that do. This differs from passive neglect: strategic abandonment involves explicit recognition that the activity once served a growth purpose. Still, it no longer does, coupled with intentional redirection of freed resources toward current developmental priorities. The professional who abandons committee membership that once built leadership skills but now merely consumes time demonstrates strategic abandonment; one who stops attending meetings without conscious evaluation demonstrates avoidance. The former creates space for aligned ambition; the latter generates guilt and fragmentation.

The ultimate integration recognizes that both ambition and contentment represent forms of engagement with life rather than attitudes toward circumstances. Contentment is not passive acceptance of unsatisfactory conditions but active appreciation of present adequacy; ambition is not frantic pursuit of missing elements but playful exploration of potential developments. Together, they enable what psychologist Carl Rogers called "fully functioning", remaining completely present in current experience while remaining open to continuous evolution. The fully functioning individual doesn't postpone satisfaction until achieving future goals, nor renounce development to protect current comfort. They recognize that sufficiency of being and the direction of becoming coexist without contradiction, that you can simultaneously be complete and evolving, that the question "Am I enough?" and the question "What might I become?" answer differently because they ask about entirely different dimensions of human experience.

Chapter 10: Environmental Sustainability: Living with Less

The climate crisis has revealed an uncomfortable mathematical reality that economists, policymakers, and ordinary citizens have largely avoided confronting: the material throughput required to maintain current consumption patterns in wealthy nations, if extended to the global population, would require approximately three to five Earths' worth of resources. This isn't speculative projection but a basic calculation derived from tracking flows of minerals, fossil fuels, fresh water, biomass, and manufactured goods through the global economy. The Global Footprint Network, which measures humanity's ecological footprint against the planet's regenerative capacity, calculates that we currently consume resources at 1.7 times the rate at which ecosystems can replenish them, essentially depleting natural capital to fund current operations. Yet this aggregate figure obscures massive inequalities in consumption patterns. The average American generates roughly four times the per-capita carbon emissions of the global average, while a resident of Bangladesh produces approximately one-twentieth as much. The mathematics becomes starker when examined through the lens of resource consumption: Australians consume approximately 35 times more natural resources per capita than residents of Mozambique. These disparities reveal that the sustainability crisis is fundamentally a crisis of excess concentrated in wealthy populations rather than a crisis of absolute human numbers. The question of environmental sustainability, therefore, collapses inevitably into questions of sufficiency: What constitutes adequate material consumption? How much is genuinely necessary for human flourishing versus culturally constructed desire? And most provocatively, can wealthy populations voluntarily reduce their resource demands to levels the planet can sustainably support, or will ecological collapse impose involuntary sufficiency through systems failure?

The Carbon Budget and the Rationing That Dare Not Speak Its Name

Climate scientists have established with uncomfortable precision that limiting global temperature rise to relatively safer levels requires humanity to emit no more than a specific remaining quantity of greenhouse gases, approximately 400 gigatons of CO_2, to maintain a reasonable probability of staying below 1.5°C warming, according to the Intergovernmental Panel on Climate Change. This finite carbon budget represents one of the clearest manifestations of planetary limits humanity has encountered. Unlike previous resource constraints that proved amenable to substitution or efficiency improvements, atmospheric chemistry operates through non-negotiable physics. Emit carbon beyond the budget, and temperatures rise regardless of economic theories, technological optimism, or political preferences. This absolute constraint forces a question that mainstream environmental discourse studiously avoids: How should a finite carbon budget be distributed among eight billion people? The answer, whether acknowledged explicitly or imposed through market mechanisms and geopolitical power, constitutes rationing. Climate policy expert Kevin Anderson at the Tyndall Centre calculates that equitable distribution of the remaining carbon budget would allocate approximately two tons of CO_2 per person annually, roughly the current emissions level of citizens in Sri Lanka or Tunisia. Americans average sixteen tons annually; Australians, twenty; Europeans, eight. Achieving equity would require reductions of 75-90% in wealthy nations, even as developing countries modestly increase their emissions to achieve basic development needs. These figures illuminate why environmental discussions obsessively focus on future technologies, carbon capture, nuclear fusion, and hydrogen economies, rather than present consumption reduction. Acknowledging that sustainability requires wealthy populations to contract their resource consumption materially confronts cultural narratives about progress, threatens economic structures dependent on growth, and demands political courage that remains conspicuously absent. Yet the carbon budget exists independent of our willingness to acknowledge it, meaning sufficiency in consumption will arrive either through conscious choice or through climate-driven catastrophes that impose involuntary reduction.

The concept of "carbon rationing" remains politically radioactive despite several nations implementing de facto versions during crises. Britain's wartime rationing system, which limited consumption of fuel, food, and manufactured goods from 1940 to 1954, demonstrated that populations could adapt to significant material constraints while maintaining social cohesion and even improving specific health indicators. Childhood nutrition actually improved during rationing periods due to more equitable food distribution. More recently, research by Yannis Dafermos at SOAS University examining carbon rationing proposals shows that tradeable personal carbon allowances, systems in which each citizen receives an equal carbon allocation that can be traded among individuals, could achieve the necessary emissions reductions while maintaining equity and consumer choice. Under such systems, individuals who choose low-carbon lifestyles (minimal flying, plant-based diets, efficient housing) could sell unused carbon credits to those requiring higher emissions, creating financial incentives for conservation while avoiding the regressive impacts of pure carbon taxation. Yet despite technical feasibility, carbon rationing proposals gain no political traction in democratic nations, mainly because they render visible what current systems obscure: that sustainability requires saying "enough" to consumption levels currently perceived as usual. The implicit rationing that occurs through market mechanisms, where carbon-intensive goods become progressively more expensive, making them accessible only to wealthy consumers, proves politically acceptable precisely because it preserves inequality while appearing to result from neutral economic forces rather than deliberate policy choices. The question facing wealthy societies is therefore not whether consumption rationing will occur, but whether it will be equitable and planned or inequitable and chaotic.

Embodied Impacts and the Visibility Problem

One of the fundamental barriers to perceiving consumption's environmental costs involves spatial and temporal displacement. The atmospheric carbon generated by charging your smartphone is produced at the power plant, potentially hundreds of miles away. The water depletion and toxic mining waste from the cobalt in your phone's battery occur in the Democratic Republic of Congo. The manufacturing pollution occurs in Shenzhen. Electronic waste accumulates in dumps in Ghana and Pakistan, where informal recyclers burn circuit boards to extract copper, releasing dioxins and heavy metals. These costs remain invisible to the consumer, who experiences only the utility of the charged device without perceiving the distributed environmental destruction its existence requires. This invisibility allows what researchers call "moral licensing", the psychological phenomenon in which taking one positive environmental action creates a perceived license to neglect others. The person who diligently recycles may feel entitled to take frequent flights; the Tesla driver may justify a large home because their vehicle is "zero emissions", conveniently ignoring the embodied carbon in battery production and the coal-fired power plants that generate the electricity used to charge their vehicle. Life cycle analysis, the methodology that tracks a product's total environmental impact from resource extraction through manufacturing, use, and disposal, consistently reveals that the majority of a product's ecological impact occurs before purchase. A cotton t-shirt requires approximately 2,700 liters of water to produce (primarily for growing cotton), generates several kilograms of CO_2 emissions during manufacturing and transport, and contains synthetic dyes derived from petrochemicals. The consumer experiences none of these impacts directly, seeing only a $15 garment whose actual environmental cost remains institutionally hidden. Making these embodied impacts visible represents one of the crucial challenges for fostering consumption sufficiency.

Some researchers advocate for comprehensive environmental labeling that would display a product's carbon footprint, water consumption, and toxicity profile at the point of purchase, similar to nutritional labeling on food. Preliminary studies by behavioral economist Jisung Park examining carbon footprint labels on consumer goods found that approximately 30% of consumers modified purchasing decisions when presented with clear environmental impact information, typically by reducing consumption rather than substituting supposedly "greener" alternatives. This finding suggests that many people already possess latent environmental values that fail to translate into behavior, primarily because the connection between consumption choices and environmental outcomes remains obscured. However, comprehensive environmental labeling faces powerful industry opposition precisely because it would reveal uncomfortable truths: that virtually all consumption in wealthy nations exceeds sustainable levels, that "eco-friendly" products often represent marginal improvements on fundamentally unsustainable practices. That genuine environmental responsibility requires a substantial reduction in total consumption rather than optimized purchasing within existing consumption levels. The resistance to environmental transparency reveals stakeholder awareness that making impacts visible would necessarily prompt questions about sufficiency, whether we need these products at all, rather than merely which version to purchase.

The Efficiency Paradox and Jevons' Law

Technological optimism about sustainability typically centers on efficiency improvements: more fuel-efficient vehicles, more energy-efficient appliances, more resource-efficient manufacturing. The implicit assumption holds that efficiency gains allow for maintained or increased consumption while reducing environmental impact. However, this assumption collides with a phenomenon that economist William Stanley Jevons identified in 1865, examining coal consumption in England. Jevons noted that improvements in steam engine efficiency, allowing each unit of coal to generate more work, led not to decreased coal consumption but to increased consumption as the improved efficiency made coal power economically attractive for more applications. This counterintuitive outcome, now termed the "Jevons Paradox" or "rebound effect," operates across virtually all efficiency improvements. More fuel-efficient vehicles make driving cheaper per mile, leading people to drive more miles; the net impact on fuel consumption is often zero or even positive. Energy-efficient LED bulbs reduce electricity costs, prompting households to install more lighting fixtures and leave lights on longer. Better insulation reduces heating costs, enabling people to maintain higher indoor temperatures or heat additional rooms. Systematic analysis by energy researcher Harry Saunders, examining efficiency improvements across multiple sectors over several decades, found rebound effects averaging 50-60%, meaning half or more of theoretical efficiency gains were consumed through increased usage rather than captured as reduced resource consumption.

The Jevons Paradox reveals a crucial insight about the relationship between efficiency and sufficiency: they operate through different, often opposing mechanisms. Efficiency optimizes how we meet needs; sufficiency questions which needs require meeting. An efficiency mindset asks, "How can we produce and consume more using fewer resources?" A sufficiency mindset asks, "How much do we actually need to produce and consume?" The former assumes current consumption levels as a fixed baseline that requires optimization; the latter treats consumption itself as a variable that requires examination. Climate scientist Kevin Anderson argues that wealthy nations have prioritized efficiency improvements for three decades while emissions have continued to rise because efficiency gains enabled expanded consumption rather than reduced impact. His analysis suggests that achieving necessary emissions reductions requires an absolute reduction in energy and material consumption among wealthy populations, with efficiency improvements playing only supplementary roles. This conclusion directly contradicts the technological optimism that dominates mainstream environmental discourse, which promises that innovation will allow maintained lifestyles with reduced impacts. The accumulated evidence increasingly suggests this promise is false, that genuine sustainability requires confronting sufficiency questions that efficiency discourse systematically evades.

Degrowth, Voluntary Simplicity, and the Sufficiency Movements

A constellation of movements has emerged explicitly advocating reduced material consumption as both an environmental necessity and a potential improvement in quality of life. The degrowth movement, strongest in European academic circles, argues that wealthy economies should intentionally contract material production and consumption while expanding non-material sources of wellbeing, social connection, creative activity, democratic participation, and ecological engagement. Degrowth scholar Giorgos Kallis frames this not as sacrifice but as liberation from the perpetual acceleration and competition that characterize growth-oriented economies. Research by environmental economist Peter Victor, modeling degrowth scenarios in Canada, suggests that managed reduction in working hours (to share employment more equitably), increased public services (to reduce individual consumption needs), progressive income redistribution, and debt cancellation could reduce greenhouse emissions by 65% while maintaining employment and slightly improving wellbeing indicators as measured by the Canadian Index of Wellbeing. These models demonstrate that sufficiency-oriented economics need not produce unemployment or poverty if transition is deliberately managed rather than imposed through crisis.

The voluntary simplicity movement, with roots in the 1970s counterculture and gaining renewed attention amid the climate crisis, advocates that individuals consciously reduce consumption and choose lifestyles that require fewer resources. Research by sociologist Duane Elgin tracking voluntary simplifiers found they typically reported higher life satisfaction despite reduced incomes, primarily because their consumption reduction was coupled with increased time for relationships, creative pursuits, and community engagement, the non-material sources of wellbeing that expanded to fill space vacated by reduced work and consumption. However, voluntary simplicity faces valid criticism as an adequate strategy for the scale of the environmental crisis. Individual choice operates within structural constraints; living car-free proves nearly impossible in cities designed around automobiles; reducing consumption when affordable housing requires two incomes becomes a luxury available primarily to those with existing wealth. Additionally, if only a minority reduces consumption while systems remain oriented toward growth, the aggregate impact remains minimal. These critiques highlight that individual sufficiency choices, while meaningful for those who make them, cannot substitute for systemic transformation that structures economies around sustainable consumption levels as the default rather than individual exception.

The concept of "sufficiency economy" promoted by Thai environmental movements offers a middle path that acknowledges both individual agency and systemic constraints. Sufficiency economy emphasizes local production for local needs, reduced dependence on global supply chains, preservation of knowledge of low-impact traditional practices, and democratic community decision-making about development priorities. Villages implementing sufficiency economy principles in rural Thailand demonstrated enhanced resilience during economic crises; their reduced integration into market economies meant global disruptions impacted them less severely than urban populations entirely dependent on commodity chains. These communities also showed substantially lower per-capita environmental impacts while maintaining adequate nutrition, healthcare access, and education outcomes.

However, translating sufficiency economy principles to urban industrial contexts proves challenging. Cities require massive resource inflows to maintain basic functions; supply chain localization faces enormous infrastructure and economic barriers; and populations acculturated to industrial consumption patterns often perceive sufficiency-oriented lifestyles as regression rather than advancement. Whether sufficiency models can scale beyond intentional communities and pilot projects to reshape mainstream urban economies remains an open and urgent question.

Planetary Boundaries and the Non-Negotiable Frame

The planetary boundaries framework, developed by Johan Rockström and colleagues at the Stockholm Resilience Centre, identifies nine Earth system processes that regulate planetary stability, climate change, biosphere integrity, land-system change, freshwater use, biogeochemical flows, ocean acidification, atmospheric aerosol loading, stratospheric ozone depletion, and novel entities (synthetic chemicals and modified organisms). The research team quantified safe operating thresholds for each process, boundaries within which human activities can continue without triggering potentially irreversible Earth system shifts. Their assessment reveals that humanity has already transgressed four boundaries (climate change, biosphere integrity, land-system change, and biogeochemical flows), operates at high risk on several others, and remains within safe limits on only two or three, depending on assessment metrics. This framework matters because it establishes that sustainability is not primarily a values question or economic optimization problem but a non-negotiable physical constraint. Operating beyond planetary boundaries for extended periods generates consequences, ecosystem collapse, climate instability, and freshwater scarcity that occur regardless of human preferences, economic arrangements, or technological capabilities. The boundaries effectively constitute Earth's "enough" threshold, the point beyond which further material extraction and waste production begin to degrade the systems that enable human civilization.

Translating planetary boundaries into individual or national consumption limits involves complex allocation questions, but broad parameters emerge from basic mathematics. Climate researcher Kimberly Nicholas calculates that maintaining climate stability requires per-capita emissions declining to approximately 2.3 tons CO_2 annually by 2030 and approaching zero by 2050. Given that the average citizen in wealthy nations currently emits 8-20 tons annually, the required reduction becomes clear: consumption patterns in the global North must contract 60-90% within one decade. These figures apply across multiple resource categories: fresh water, biomass, minerals, and synthetic nitrogen. Research mapping consumption patterns to planetary boundaries by environmental scientist Daniel O'Neill found that no nation currently provides high material living standards for its citizens while operating within planetary boundaries. This finding demolishes the assumption that sustainability merely requires technical optimization; it reveals that prevailing definitions of adequate living standards in wealthy nations are ecologically impossible to universalize or maintain. The planetary boundaries framework, therefore, forces an uncomfortable conclusion: wealthy populations face not an optimization problem but a reduction imperative. Sufficiency ceases being an optional lifestyle preference and becomes a biophysical necessity.

This non-negotiable frame transforms environmental discourse by eliminating the false comfort that innovation or efficiency might allow maintained consumption patterns.

When boundaries are transgressed, systems respond through their own logic, algae blooms spread across fertilizer-contaminated waterways regardless of economic impacts on adjacent communities; glaciers melt according to thermodynamics rather than political convenience. The Earth system operates without consideration for human preferences, meaning our choices reduce to whether we consciously organize societies around sustainable consumption levels or whether Earth system feedbacks impose sufficiency involuntarily through agricultural collapse, freshwater scarcity, and climate instability that render current consumption patterns physically impossible. Framing sustainability through planetary boundaries shifts the question from "How much reduction can we politically accept?" to "How do we equitably organize human societies within the resource budgets biophysical reality has established?" This reframing proves politically challenging because it renders visible what economic systems obscure: that wealth accumulation in affluent nations depends on resource consumption levels that breach planetary boundaries, meaning current inequality is not merely unjust but physically unsustainable.

From Individual Virtue to Structural Transformation

The relationship between individual consumption choices and systemic environmental outcomes remains contested. Environmental advocates often promote personal actions, such as reducing meat consumption, avoiding single-use plastics, installing solar panels, and purchasing offsets, as meaningful contributions to sustainability. Critics dismiss these as inadequate individualist responses to structural problems requiring policy transformation and corporate accountability. This debate obscures a more nuanced reality:

individual actions are necessary but radically insufficient without structural change, while structural change will ultimately prove politically impossible without cultural shifts in consumption expectations that must begin, at least partially, through individual choices. The challenge involves neither pure individualism nor pure structuralism but understanding how they interact. Research by social psychologist Thomas Dietz examining pro-environmental behaviors found that individual actions, even when adopted widely, typically reduce household environmental impacts by 20-30%, a significant but clearly inadequate reduction given the 60-90% reductions required for sustainability. However, the same research found that individuals who adopted voluntary consumption reduction became significantly more likely to support aggressive environmental policies, join activist organizations, and vote based on climate positions. Individual behavior change created political constituency for structural transformation, suggesting these levels interact rather than substitute for each other.

The narrative that individualizes environmental responsibility, that the climate crisis results from consumers making poor choices, serves industries that benefit from deflecting attention from corporate emissions and lobbying against systemic regulations. British Petroleum's promotion of "carbon footprint" calculators exemplifies this strategy, positioning climate responsibility as an individual consumer problem while BP continued extracting fossil fuels at scale. Yet the countervailing narrative that personal choices are meaningless in the face of corporate power risks promoting passivity. Most corporate emissions ultimately serve consumer demand, fossil fuel companies extract oil because people drive, and industrial agriculture expands because people eat meat. Fast fashion proliferates because people purchase disposable clothing. Distinguishing genuine need from manufactured demand proves difficult, but claiming all consumption is imposed removes individual agency in ways that seem empirically false. People do choose between driving and cycling, between meat-based and plant-based diets, and between fast fashion and clothing repair. The synthesis involves recognizing that individual choices matter but occur within structural constraints that policy must address. Person A cannot easily choose car-free living in a city designed without public transit, but citizens collectively can demand transit investment. Person B faces difficulty reducing meat consumption when affordable food options center on animal products, but voters can support agricultural policies favoring plant-based protein. Individual and structural change form feedback loops rather than either-or alternatives.

Environmental sustainability, grounded in sufficiency, therefore requires simultaneous transformation at multiple levels. Individual examination of "How much is enough?" becomes meaningful only within communities and political systems that structurally support sustainable consumption levels as a default rather than an exceptional choice requiring extraordinary effort. A parent who examines whether their child truly needs new clothing or can wear hand-me-downs engages in a valuable sufficiency practice. Still, this choice proves far easier in social contexts where children are not bullied for wearing used clothing and where school dress cultures do not require constant fashion conformity. Similarly, policy interventions that make sustainable choices the default, dense, walkable urban development, comprehensive public transit, and progressive carbon taxation prove more effective than policies that require continuous individual decision-making against systemic pressures toward consumption. The environmental crisis demands both personal interrogation of sufficiency and collective restructuring of systems that currently define adequacy through ecologically impossible consumption levels.

The convergence of the climate crisis, biodiversity collapse, and transgressed planetary boundaries creates unprecedented urgency to translate sufficiency from an abstract concept into lived practice at scale. The mathematics are uncomfortably clear: maintaining Earth systems that enable human flourishing requires wealthy populations to rapidly and substantially reduce material consumption. This necessity exists independent of whether it feels politically possible, economically convenient, or culturally acceptable. The question facing contemporary societies is therefore not whether consumption will decrease but whether that decrease will be consciously chosen and equitably distributed or chaotically imposed through environmental collapse that destroys the resource base upon which all human activities depend. Living with less is not, ultimately, a lifestyle choice but an inevitable consequence of living on a finite planet whose limits we have reached. How we navigate that transition, whether toward dystopian scarcity or toward lives that prove "less but better", contains genuinely more satisfaction than the exhausting abundance that characterizes our current, unsustainable moment.

Chapter 11: Enough in the Digital Age: Managing Information Overload

The human brain processes visual information at approximately 10 million bits per second, yet conscious awareness handles only about 40-50 bits per second, a reduction factor of roughly 200,000 to one. For most of evolutionary history, this filtering presented no challenge. The information available to our ancestors remained constrained by physical proximity and the limits of human memory. A person might encounter several dozen distinct pieces of information daily: observations about weather patterns, interactions with community members, changes in local flora and fauna, and stories shared around evening fires. Today, a single scroll through a social media feed exposes us to more novel information in five minutes than a medieval person encountered in a month. A 2020 study by researchers at the University of California, San Diego, calculated that Americans consume approximately 34 gigabytes of information daily, the equivalent of reading 174 full-length newspapers. This represents a 350% increase from data consumption levels measured in 1980. Yet the neurological architecture processing this deluge has not changed in the intervening forty years, much less the intervening forty thousand years since our cognitive equipment evolved. We are processing twenty-first-century information volumes through Paleolithic wetware, creating a fundamental mismatch between system capacity and demand that manifests as diffuse anxiety, scattered attention, and a perpetual sense of being overwhelmed, characterizing contemporary digital existence. The question of "enough" in information consumption involves not merely personal preference but cognitive sustainability, determining how much information the human mind can meaningfully process before the filtering mechanisms break down entirely and consciousness becomes mere noise.

The information economy operates on fundamentally different principles than material economies, creating unique challenges for determining sufficiency. Physical goods obey laws of scarcity and thermodynamics; consuming food removes it from availability, and using gasoline converts it to exhaust. Information defies these constraints. Reading this paragraph does not prevent others from reading it; downloading a song does not diminish the original. Economist Paul Romer won the Nobel Prize partially for formalizing how information goods enable increasing returns rather than diminishing returns. Each additional user adds value to the network without depleting the resource. This abundance creates the paradoxical problem called "attention scarcity." While information itself proliferates infinitely, human attention remains absolutely finite. Netflix currently offers approximately 15,000 hours of content; watching it all would require 625 days of continuous viewing without sleep. Spotify contains over 80 million songs, which would need 548 years to hear once each. Steam offers more than 50,000 video games, representing roughly 3.5 million hours of gameplay. No individual will ever experience more than an infinitesimal fraction of available content, meaning our relationship with digital media necessarily involves perpetual exclusion. Unlike physical scarcity, where I cannot afford the house I want, digital abundance creates what philosopher Ruth Chang calls "hard choices," where no objectively correct answer exists because options are incomparable rather than insufficient. The cognitive burden of perpetually navigating an infinite number of possibilities without clear selection criteria generates what psychologist Barry Schwartz terms "the paradox of choice," in which expanded options correlate with decreased satisfaction. Research by Schwartz and colleagues found that participants who were asked to choose chocolates from an array of six options reported higher satisfaction with their selection than those who chose from a larger variety of 30 options, despite the larger set theoretically increasing the probability of finding an optimal match. This pattern replicates across digital contexts: streaming services with vast libraries correlate with longer browsing times and lower viewing satisfaction than limited-channel television; dating apps offering thousands of potential partners correlate with lower relationship formation than environments with constrained options. The sufficiency question in digital contexts, therefore, inverts: rather than asking "Do I have access to enough information?" we must ask "How do I select enough information from infinite availability to remain cognitively functional?"

The Attention Economy and Manufactured Insufficiency

Digital platforms engineer insufficiency through psychological mechanisms so sophisticated that they make traditional advertising appear crude by comparison. The fundamental business model underlying "free" digital services, social media, search engines, video platforms, and news aggregators involves capturing attention and selling it to advertisers. This creates perverse incentives in which platform success depends on maximizing time-on-site, screen interactions, and emotional engagement, regardless of whether these serve user well-being. Former design ethicist Tristan Harris, who worked at Google before becoming a prominent critic of attention exploitation, revealed how platforms employ "hijacking techniques" derived from behavioral psychology and neuroscience. Variable reward schedules, the exact mechanism underlying slot machine addiction, determine when social media platforms deliver notifications, prompting users to check whether "this time" yields engaging content repeatedly. Infinite scroll eliminates natural stopping points that would allow users to decide whether to continue consciously, instead creating frictionless progression until external interruptions force disengagement. Autoplay features ensure content consumption continues without requiring active choice, converting passive non-objection into continued engagement. Read receipts and "last seen" indicators on messaging platforms create social pressure for immediate response, transforming asynchronous communication into functionally synchronous demands. These mechanisms share a typical architecture: they reduce the cognitive effort required to continue consuming while increasing the effort needed to stop, exactly inverting the friction distribution that would support autonomous sufficiency determinations.

The sophistication escalates through algorithmic curation systems that learn individual vulnerability patterns and exploit them systematically. Recommendation algorithms track not just what content users choose but also how long they engage, where they pause or rewatch, what they skip, and what emotional reactions they exhibit (measured through engagement patterns, linguistic analysis of comments, and, increasingly, device sensors detecting ambient noise and facial expressions). This data trains machine learning models to optimize for "engagement", a euphemistic metric that correlates strongly with emotional arousal, especially negative emotions like outrage, anxiety, and fear, which are more engaging than contentment or calm. Research by data scientist Guillaume Chaslot, who worked on YouTube's recommendation algorithm, revealed that the system systematically steers viewers toward increasingly extreme content because extreme material generates stronger engagement signals. A user researching a medical condition would progressively receive recommendations for more alarming diagnoses, conspiracy theories about pharmaceutical companies, and alternative treatments with dubious efficacy, not because these provide accurate information but because they maximize viewing time. The algorithm functions as an amoral optimization machine, indifferent to content accuracy or user well-being, concerned exclusively with the objective function programmed into it: maximize engagement metrics. Users experience this as the platform "understanding" their interests, when more accurately, the system has identified their psychological vulnerabilities and exploited them for commercial advantage. The fundamental asymmetry involves users making conscious choices with limited information and cognitive resources. At the same time, platforms deploy teams of engineers, vast datasets, and machine learning systems optimized through billions of interactions to subvert those choices. This represents not merely advertising but automated psychological manipulation at scale, making autonomous sufficiency determinations nearly impossible.

Information Triage and the Necessity of Strategic Ignorance

Dealing with information abundance requires developing what library scientists call "information literacy", the capacity to effectively locate, evaluate, and use information sources. However, traditional information literacy assumes scarcity contexts in which the challenge is finding relevant information amid limited resources. Contemporary challenges involve the opposite problem: filtering relevant information from overwhelming abundance. This requires a fundamentally different skill set that educators have barely begun to address. Journalist and author Rolf Dobelli argues that the most valuable information skill in the digital age is "strategic ignorance", the deliberate cultivation of specific areas of non-knowledge. Dobelli quit consuming news entirely in 2010, arguing that the news creates an illusion of understanding while delivering primarily irrelevant or misleading information unsuitable for decision-making. His framework distinguishes between "relevant to my life and within my control," "relevant to my life but outside my control," "irrelevant to my life but within my control," and "irrelevant to my life and outside my control." News overwhelmingly falls into the final category, information about events that neither affect us personally nor respond to our actions, yet consumes attention disproportionate to its utility. A factory fire in Bangladesh, a political scandal in a distant nation, a celebrity divorce, a rare disease affecting a dozen people globally, these stories generate attention and emotional response despite having zero bearing on the choices available to most consumers. News organizations defend this by invoking civic responsibility and informed citizenry. Still, research by communications scholar Markus Prior, examining news consumption patterns and political knowledge, found no correlation between news consumption volume and informed voting behavior, while finding a strong correlation between news consumption and anxiety levels. The information provides minimal decision-relevant knowledge while imposing significant emotional costs.

Strategic ignorance extends beyond news to encompass most digital information streams. Email newsletters, social media feeds, messaging groups, podcast subscriptions, YouTube channels, and blog updates collectively generate more content daily than any individual could consume in weeks. The default approach involves attempting to "keep up", processing everything that arrives, experiencing perpetual backlog anxiety about unconsumed content, and feeling overwhelmed by unmanageable volume. The alternative involves consciously defining sufficiency thresholds and systematically ignoring everything beyond them. This requires confronting uncomfortable truths about digital FOMO (fear of missing out). What if something important happens that you miss? The reality: important information typically reaches you through multiple channels over time, while truly urgent information requiring immediate response is scarce. Missing a trending topic, not seeing friends' social media updates, and being unaware of some controversy animating online discourse create no meaningful consequences beyond temporary social awkwardness. Research by media psychologist Elly Konijn examining FOMO and information anxiety found that participants randomly assigned to reduce social media consumption by 50% for one month reported decreased anxiety and increased life satisfaction, while reporting that they had missed "nothing important" during their reduced engagement period. The fear of missing out proves largely illusory, a manufactured anxiety exploited by platforms rather than a realistic assessment of the importance of information. Developing strategic ignorance involves consciously rejecting the premise that more information produces better outcomes, instead recognizing that beyond relatively low sufficiency thresholds, additional information generates noise that degrades rather than enhances decision quality.

The information triage process requires explicit criteria for filtering. Medical triage in emergency departments uses clear protocols: life-threatening conditions receive immediate attention, serious but stable conditions wait briefly, minor issues wait indefinitely, and some conditions (like common colds) are redirected elsewhere entirely. Information triage needs comparable clarity. One framework involves distinguishing "need to know," "useful to know," and "interesting to know," then ruthlessly filtering everything beyond the first category until that category is fully addressed. For most people, "need to know" information occupies perhaps 5% of information actually consumed, "useful to know" another 15%, and "interesting to know" the remaining 80%. Inverting that distribution, spending 80% of information time on need-to-know material, would dramatically improve decision quality while freeing enormous time and attention. Another framework involves temporal prioritization: information relevant to decisions being made this week receives attention; information pertinent to someday-maybe decisions gets archived unread; information relevant to no decisions gets deleted unread. This doesn't prove easy because it requires admitting that we cannot, and need not, know everything, cannot maintain expertise across all domains, and must accept that vast territories of human knowledge will remain permanently beyond our awareness. In pre-digital eras, these limitations were imposed automatically by physical constraints. The shift to digital abundance makes previously automatic filtering a conscious responsibility requiring deliberate practice and psychological adjustment. The emotional difficulty involved in deleting unread emails, leaving notifications unchecked, and letting information opportunities pass suggests how deeply the "never miss anything" orientation has penetrated contemporary consciousness, despite its apparent impossibility.

The Quality-Quantity Inversion and Deep Engagement

The economics of attention scarcity and information abundance create systematic bias toward breadth over depth. Digital platforms maximize profitability by maximizing the number of content exposures, creating incentives for users to consume many pieces briefly rather than a few pieces thoroughly. An article read superficially generates advertising impressions; an article pondered deeply generates the same impressions without additional engagement metrics. This creates what media theorist Nicholas Carr calls "the shallows", digital environments that train scatter-shot attention patterns while atrophying capacities for sustained concentration. Carr documents how his own reading patterns shifted after decades of internet use. Where he once read books for hours without interruption, he found himself unable to maintain focus for more than a few pages before craving digital stimulation. Neuroscience research supports these observations. Brain imaging studies by UCLA psychiatrist Gary Small found measurable differences in neural activation patterns between "digital natives" (those growing up with the internet) and "digital immigrants" (those adopting it as adults), particularly in regions associated with decision-making and complex reasoning. Digital natives showed reduced activation in prefrontal cortex regions during text reading compared to immigrants, suggesting different, arguably less thorough, processing of written material. The technology literally rewires neural architecture in ways that favor rapid content switching over deep engagement.

This creates a sufficiency paradox: consuming more information may reduce rather than increase understanding. Genuine comprehension of complex topics requires sustained attention, allowing concepts to integrate, questions to emerge, and connections to form. Reading a thoughtful 8,000-word essay on climate policy generates more understanding than skimming fifty brief articles on the same topic. Yet, the latter feels more productive because it exposes us to more sources. Research by cognitive psychologist Daniel Willingham, examining reading comprehension, found that understanding complex material requires approximately 15 minutes of sustained focus for neural networks encoding concepts to stabilize. Interruptions during this period, notifications, message checks, and browser tab switches disrupt encoding and require restarting the focus period. Given that research by Microsoft scientist Linda Stone on digital device usage found that the average knowledge worker switches tasks every 3 minutes and checks email every 5 minutes, the neural requirements for genuine comprehension are systematically violated throughout typical digital days. We're perpetually in the first five minutes of understanding something, never reaching the neural state where genuine learning occurs. The solution involves inverting the quality-quantity ratio: consuming far fewer information sources while engaging each thoroughly enough for comprehension. Practically, this might mean reading three carefully chosen long-form articles weekly rather than skimming thirty brief ones, or following two genuinely informative blogs rather than maintaining fifty feed subscriptions generating hundreds of unread items. This substitution proves psychologically challenging because it produces less visible activity; the person reading one book appears to accomplish less than the person posting about twelve books they've started, yet generates dramatically superior cognitive outcomes.

Digital Sabbath and the Architecture of Disconnection

Religious traditions developed Sabbath practices millennia before digital technology, yet their psychological insights apply with renewed force to contemporary information overload. The Jewish Shabbat prohibits creative work from Friday sunset to Saturday sunset, creating a weekly rhythm between engagement and rest. The practice recognizes that continuous productivity degrades both output quality and human well-being, and that restoration requires not merely reduced activity but categorical disengagement from production-oriented consciousness. Christian traditions developed similar Sunday observances, Muslim practice includes Jummah, focused on community and spiritual reflection, and Buddhist monastic schedules include regular meditation retreats from worldly concerns. These traditions share recognition that humans require regular, substantial disconnection from ordinary consciousness patterns to maintain psychological health and clarity. The digital age demands parallel practices but faces greater challenges because digital connection penetrates every domain. Pre-digital Sabbath occurred automatically when one left the workplace; digital connectivity means work follows us home, into bed, on vacation, and into every formerly protected space. Creating meaningful disconnection, therefore, requires deliberate architecture rather than relying on default separation.

Digital Sabbath practices vary widely but share the core principle of scheduled, extended disconnection from digital information streams. Some practitioners adopt weekly device-free days; others implement daily digital sunset hours; some create device-free zones (bedrooms, dining tables) rather than device-free times. The specific structure matters less than consistency and genuine commitment. Research by neuroscientist Adam Gazzaley examining meditation practices and attention restoration found that benefits accrued primarily when practices occurred regularly and for substantial periods; brief, sporadic disconnection provided minimal benefit. In contrast, consistent daily practice of 30+ minutes showed measurable improvements in attention control and working memory. Applied to digital Sabbath, this suggests that twenty-minute phone-free periods scattered randomly provide less benefit than a consistently observed three-hour evening disconnection or a whole weekend day offline. The challenge involves defending these boundaries against both external pressure (work expectations, social obligations) and internal impulses

(FOMO, habit, boredom). Technology writer Nir Eyal recommends "precommitment strategies", advanced decisions that remove choice from moments of temptation. These might include giving one's phone to a friend during Sabbath hours, using outlet timers that automatically disconnect home WiFi at designated times, or deleting social media apps from devices (requiring login through browser, adding friction to access). The goal is to make disconnection the default that requires no willpower to maintain, rather than a constant battle for access.

The deeper challenge involves confronting what disconnection reveals. Many people discover that removing digital distraction exposes underlying emotional states, boredom, loneliness, and anxiety that chronic connectivity was masking. Psychologist Larry Rosen's research on "nomophobia" (no-mobile-phone phobia) found that participants separated from phones for even one hour experienced measurable anxiety increases, with symptoms including restlessness, elevated heart rate, and intrusive thoughts about potential missed messages. This suggests digital connection functions partly as anxiolytic self-medication, a mechanism for avoiding difficult internal experiences rather than merely accessing information. The irony: digital overconsumption often stems from attempts to escape negative emotions it itself generates, creating a vicious cycle in which the solution exacerbates the problem. Breaking this pattern requires not just scheduling disconnection but developing alternative strategies for managing the emotions that surface during disconnected periods. This might involve meditation practices, physical exercise, creative activities, face-to-face social interaction, or simply learning to tolerate boredom without immediately reaching for stimulation. Contemplative traditions suggest that the capacity to remain present with unpleasant internal states, rather than constantly seeking distraction, represents a crucial psychological skill enabling both well-being and genuine choice. Digital Sabbath, approached seriously, becomes less about information management and more about developing the internal resources necessary to exist contentedly without constant external stimulation.

The Algorithmic Self and Identity Fragmentation

Digital platforms don't merely distribute information; they construct versions of who we are based on data we generate, then reflect these constructions to us in ways that shape subsequent behavior. Every search query, purchase, click, pause, and scroll feeds algorithms that build probabilistic models predicting our preferences, vulnerabilities, and future behaviors. These models then determine what content we encounter: which products appear in shopping feeds, which posts surface on social media, which videos autoplay next, and which news stories reach our awareness. We experience this curation as the platform "knowing" us, but the algorithmic model of our identity bears an ambiguous relationship to our actual selves. The model captures patterns in past behavior while remaining ignorant of context, intention, values, or aspirations that make behavior meaningful. Amazon's recommendation system knows I purchased a pregnancy test but not whether the result was wanted; it knows I bought moving boxes but not whether the relocation was chosen or forced; it knows I researched cancer treatments but not whether the patient survived. The algorithm treats all signals as equal inputs while remaining structurally incapable of understanding the meanings that make some signals revealing and others misleading. This creates what technology theorist Jaron Lanier calls "the algorithmic self", a reductive data portrait that platforms treat as who we are, increasingly determining what information and opportunities we encounter.

The recursive feedback creates identity fragmentation and reinforcement. Suppose algorithms detect that I've clicked several articles about anxiety. In that case, they feed me more anxiety-related content, which I consume because it's offered, which strengthens the algorithmic assessment that I'm interested in anxiety, generating more anxiety content in an escalating spiral. The person experiencing temporary stress becomes algorithmically categorized as someone defined by anxiety, then receives information flows reinforcing this identity until the algorithmic fiction shapes reality. Similar dynamics operate across domains: someone who watches a few gaming videos becomes algorithmically a "gamer" and receives exclusively gaming-related recommendations, potentially foreclosing exposure to other interests; someone who clicks on political content receives increasingly partisan material as the algorithm optimizes for engagement by feeding existing orientations rather than broadening perspective. Research by data scientist Renee DiResta examining radicalization patterns on YouTube found that the recommendation algorithm created "rabbit holes" where users interested in relatively mainstream content received progressively more extreme recommendations because extreme content generated stronger engagement signals. The algorithm doesn't care about accuracy or user well-being; it simply optimizes its objective function by steering users toward whatever content historically maximized their engagement, regardless of whether this serves their stated interests or values.

This creates profound challenges for autonomous identity formation and for determining sufficiency. If the information we encounter is algorithmically curated based on past behavior, and if that info influences future behavior, we're caught in feedback loops where algorithms increasingly determine not just what we know but who we become. The question "Have I consumed enough information on this topic?" becomes unanswerable because the information presented has been filtered through opaque systems designed to maximize engagement rather than support informed decision-making. Breaking these loops requires conscious intervention: deliberately seeking information the algorithm wouldn't surface, regularly purging watch histories and cookies to reset algorithmic profiles, using search engines and platforms that don't personalize results, and recognizing that default information flows are curated rather than comprehensive. Some practitioners advocate for what technologist Eli Pariser calls "filter bubble" audits, periodically using different platforms, browsers, and search tools to see what information appears when one's profile isn't guiding curation, revealing how constrained the algorithmically-curated view has become. These audits consistently demonstrate that the information environment one experiences bears limited resemblance to what others encounter or what comprehensive research would discover. Each user inhabits a customized information universe optimized for engagement rather than accuracy or comprehensiveness.

The philosophical implications extend beyond practical inconvenience. If personal identity involves the stories we tell about ourselves, the knowledge we accumulate, and the perspectives we hold, and if these are increasingly shaped by algorithmic systems we don't control operating according to objectives misaligned with our interests, then contemporary selfhood involves a kind of colonization where corporate optimization functions partially construct our inner lives. This represents a historically unprecedented threat to autonomy, making questions about information sufficiency inseparable from those about the conditions necessary for authentic selfhood. We cannot meaningfully determine "enough" when the information determining that judgment has been systematically curated to keep us consuming. Reclaiming autonomous sufficiency determination requires not just better personal habits but collective resistance to the business models and technological architectures that profit from perpetual insufficiency.

The path toward information sufficiency in the digital age requires recognizing that current information environments are not neutral tools but are systematically designed to maximize consumption regardless of cognitive costs or lived well-being. Platform designers, advertisers, and content creators all benefit from perpetual engagement, creating aligned incentives to subvert our capacity for autonomous sufficiency determination. Genuine agency requires understanding these dynamics and consciously constructing alternative information architectures: scheduled disconnection, aggressive filtering, quality-over-quantity inversion, and recognition that missing information opportunities represent not personal failure but necessary prioritization in contexts of abundance. The challenge exceeds individual discipline; it requires collective pressure on platforms to align their business models with user wellbeing, regulatory frameworks to prevent manipulative design, and a cultural revaluation of scattered distraction toward focused engagement. Until these shifts occur, navigating information sufficiency remains an exercise in swimming against deliberately engineered currents designed to keep us forever overwhelmed, forever consuming, and forever just one click away from enough.

Chapter 12: Health and Wellness: Recognizing Bodily Sufficiency

The human body maintains approximately 37 trillion cells, each executing thousands of chemical reactions per second to sustain the intricate equilibrium we call health. This biological machinery operates through feedback mechanisms so sophisticated that conscious intervention often proves counterproductive. Yet contemporary wellness culture has convinced millions that their bodies require constant optimization, perpetual monitoring, and aggressive intervention to achieve states the organism would naturally maintain if given adequate conditions and left reasonably alone. The fitness tracker market alone generated $36.3 billion globally in 2020, with projections reaching $114 billion by 2028, an industry premised on the assumption that bodily function requires external measurement and correction. Walk through any affluent neighborhood and observe runners checking heart rate monitors every 30 seconds, cyclists analyzing power output metrics in real time, and even casual walkers tracking step counts as though their legs might forget how to ambulate without digital verification. This obsessive quantification reflects a fundamental distrust of somatic intelligence, the body's innate capacity to regulate itself, that parallels the broader cultural inability to recognize sufficiency. The person who cannot trust their body to signal genuine hunger versus psychological craving, who cannot distinguish between fatigue requiring rest and discomfort indicating beneficial adaptation, who needs an app to confirm whether they slept adequately despite being the only consciousness with direct access to that information, has lost connection with the most fundamental feedback system available to human awareness. This disconnection from bodily sufficiency generates a peculiar form of alienation: estrangement from the very organism we inhabit.

The medical establishment bears significant responsibility for cultivating this distrust by pathologizing normal variation in human physiology and functioning. Blood pressure guidelines have been progressively lowered over decades, transforming millions of previously healthy individuals into patients requiring pharmaceutical intervention. The threshold for hypertension dropped from 160/100 in the 1970s to 140/90 in subsequent decades, and to 130/80 as of the 2017 American Heart Association guidelines. Each revision expanded the patient population by millions, despite limited evidence that treatment of these lower thresholds produces meaningful health improvements for most individuals. A similar pattern characterizes cholesterol guidelines, glucose tolerance ranges, and bone density thresholds, where narrowing definitions of normal convert statistical variation into medical conditions requiring intervention. Physician H. Gilbert Welch's research examining cancer screening programs reveals how detecting abnormalities that would never cause symptoms or harm during a person's natural lifespan, a phenomenon called overdiagnosis, has become epidemic. Thyroid cancer diagnoses increased threefold between 1975 and 2009, yet mortality remained unchanged, suggesting that vast numbers of people received cancer diagnoses and underwent surgery for conditions that posed no actual threat. The body contained cellular irregularities that fell within the spectrum of normal biological variation, but the medicalization of increasingly sensitive detection technology transformed these variations into diseases requiring treatment. This pattern reveals an uncomfortable reality: much of contemporary medical intervention addresses not actual bodily insufficiency but rather the insufficiency of human tolerance for uncertainty and variation.

The Tyranny of Optimal Health

The concept of health itself has undergone a transformation that makes it nearly impossible to recognize bodily sufficiency. The World Health Organization's 1948 definition characterized health as "a state of complete physical, mental, and social well-being and not merely the absence of disease or infirmity." While aspirational, this definition set an impossible standard, complete well-being in all domains simultaneously, that ensures perpetual inadequacy. No human being at any point in history has achieved or could achieve this state. More problematically, the definition shifts health from a relative condition (adequate function given one's age, genetic inheritance, and circumstances) to an absolute standard that admits infinite degrees of insufficiency. If health means complete well-being, then any sub-optimal state constitutes ill health requiring intervention. The emergence of "wellness" as distinct from health represents this perfectionist drift taken to its logical extreme. Wellness discourse no longer concerns itself with treating disease or maintaining function but rather with optimizing performance, appearance, and longevity to hypothetical maximums. The wellness industry, encompassing supplements, fitness programs, alternative therapies, biohacking technologies, and longevity interventions, generated over $4.4 trillion globally in 2020, dwarfing the conventional medical sector. This industry operates on the principle of manufacturing inadequacy: identifying metrics that can continually be improved (muscle mass, aerobic capacity, cognitive speed, inflammatory markers, mitochondrial density) and positioning improvement as a moral imperative rather than an optional enhancement.

Biohacking communities exemplify this optimization mindset taken to extremes. Practitioners measure dozens of biomarkers weekly, modulate sleep through lighting manipulation and pharmaceutical intervention, consume elaborate supplement protocols containing thirty or more compounds, practice severe caloric restriction or ketogenic diets intended to trigger cellular stress responses, undergo cryotherapy and infrared sauna exposure to manipulate metabolic function, and inject themselves with experimental peptides and hormones to enhance various physiological parameters. The underlying assumption is that the body's default operations are not sufficiently optimized and require aggressive external management to achieve optimal performance. Yet longitudinal health outcomes data for these practices remain largely absent; the interventions are too recent for meaningful long-term assessment, meaning practitioners conduct uncontrolled experiments on themselves in pursuit of hypothetical benefits that may never materialize or may be offset by harms that won't manifest for decades. More fundamentally, this approach treats the body as a machine requiring constant tuning rather than as a self-regulating system that maintains equilibrium when provided adequate inputs and protected from genuine threats. The biohacker, examining their continuous glucose monitor every fifteen minutes and calculating optimal meal timing based on glycemic response, has lost sight of a crucial reality: humans successfully regulated blood glucose for 300,000 years without such monitoring through simple mechanisms like feeling hungry when energy was needed and satiated when sufficient fuel was consumed. The body knows how to be a body; the question is whether we trust it enough to let it perform that function.

Interoception and the Wisdom of Bodily Signals

The scientific understanding of interoception, the perception of internal bodily states, reveals capacities far more sophisticated than wellness culture acknowledges. Neuroscientist Bud Craig's research mapping interoceptive pathways identified dedicated neural systems that continuously monitor internal conditions: blood oxygen levels, nutrient availability, hydration status, tissue damage, immune activation, gut microbiome activity, hormonal fluctuations, and dozens of other parameters. These systems integrate information into coherent representations of bodily state that emerge as feelings, urges, and intuitions guiding behavior. Hunger signals metabolic need; thirst indicates hydration deficit; fatigue suggests accumulated sleep debt or overtraining; pain localizes tissue damage; nausea warns of ingested toxins. When functioning correctly, interoceptive awareness provides real-time feedback about bodily sufficiency across multiple domains without requiring conscious analysis or external measurement. The person with intact interoceptive capacity knows they've eaten enough when satiety signals register, knows they've rested enough when energy returns, and knows they've trained sufficiently when performance plateaus or declines. This internal monitoring system proves remarkably accurate when trusted and cultivated, yet contemporary culture systematically undermines interoceptive development through interventions that override or ignore bodily signals.

Children learn to distrust interoceptive cues when forced to finish meals despite satiety signals, when required to maintain rigid sleep schedules despite varying sleep needs, and when pushed to continue athletic activity despite pain signals indicating injury risk. Adults extend this distrust by consuming stimulants to override fatigue rather than addressing sleep debt, taking analgesics to mask pain rather than modifying activities that generate tissue stress, and eating according to external schedules or nutritional calculations rather than genuine hunger and satiety cues. The quantified-self movement represents the ultimate externalization of bodily knowledge, replacing interoceptive awareness with digital proxies that supposedly provide more reliable information than consciousness itself can access. Yet research comparing interoceptive accuracy (how well people perceive their actual bodily states) with objective measurements reveals that trained interoceptive awareness rivals or exceeds device accuracy for many parameters. Studies by Sarah Garfinkel at the University of Sussex found that individuals trained in body-scanning meditation could estimate their heart rate within 2-3 beats per minute on average without pulse monitoring, comparable to the accuracy of consumer wearables. More significantly, high interoceptive awareness correlated with better emotional regulation, lower anxiety, and improved decision-making across domains, suggesting that trusting bodily signals enhances overall functioning beyond the specific physiological parameters monitored. The person who knows when they've had enough to eat doesn't merely avoid overconsumption; they develop a generalized capacity to recognize sufficiency across contexts.

Movement Sufficiency and the Exercise Trap

Physical activity is a domain where recognizing enough is particularly challenging, as cultural messages consistently suggest that more exercise invariably produces better outcomes. Athletic performance culture venerates training volume and intensity, celebrating individuals who push past exhaustion and normalize pain as weakness, leaving the body. Recreational fitness has adopted this mindset: marathon runners meticulously log weekly mileage, weightlifters track progressive overload, and CrossFit participants compete on benchmarks for workout volume and intensity. The underlying assumption holds that adaptation requires perpetually escalating challenge, that maintenance of fitness necessitates continued progression, and that backing off represents regression or insufficient commitment. Yet exercise physiology research reveals a more nuanced reality: adaptation occurs during recovery periods following training stimulus, not during the exercise itself. Overtraining syndrome, characterized by performance decline, persistent fatigue, hormonal disruption, immune suppression, and psychological symptoms, results from insufficient recovery relative to training stress. The body adapts when training stimulus remains within its capacity to repair and strengthen tissues; exceeding that capacity produces cumulative damage rather than enhanced fitness. This creates a threshold where sufficient exercise generates health benefits while excessive exercise produces physiological harm, yet identifying that threshold requires interoceptive sensitivity that many athletes have systematically suppressed.

Research by Tim Noakes examining endurance athletes identified what he termed the "central governor theory", that fatigue during extreme exertion results from brain-imposed limitations designed to prevent catastrophic physiological damage rather than from actual muscular energy depletion. The brain monitors multiple homeostatic parameters and generates overwhelming fatigue signals when continued exertion risks genuine harm. Elite endurance culture teaches athletes to override these signals, treating discomfort as mental weakness to be conquered through psychological toughness. Yet athletes who consistently override the central governor suffer higher rates of sudden cardiac events, rhabdomyolysis (muscle tissue breakdown, releasing proteins that damage the kidneys), and long-term endocrine dysfunction. The body's signals indicating enough exercise has occurred serve protective functions; ignoring them in pursuit of performance gains or caloric expenditure targets reflects the same distrust of somatic intelligence evident across wellness culture. Meanwhile, epidemiological research consistently demonstrates that health benefits from exercise plateau relatively early; 150 minutes of moderate activity weekly yield the most significant achievable reductions in mortality and disease prevention, with diminishing returns beyond that threshold and potential harm at extreme volumes. The person running 80 miles weekly achieves no meaningful longevity advantage over the person maintaining 20-30 miles weekly, but incurs substantially higher injury risk and time cost. Recognizing movement sufficiency requires acknowledging that exercise serves health maintenance rather than infinite optimization, and that adequate function rather than maximal performance constitutes a legitimate goal.

Nutritional Agnosticism and the Diet Industry's False Promises

Few domains generate more confusion about sufficiency than nutrition, where competing dietary philosophies make mutually exclusive claims about optimal eating patterns. Low-fat advocates warn that dietary fat causes cardiovascular disease and obesity; ketogenic proponents argue that carbohydrates are toxins producing metabolic dysfunction; carnivore dieters claim plant compounds are anti-nutrients that harm human health; vegans insist animal products cause cancer and inflammatory diseases. Each position marshals research, testimonials, and mechanistic rationales to support their recommendations while dismissing contradictory evidence. This cacophony creates decision paralysis for individuals simply trying to identify adequate nutrition, transforming the straightforward question of eating enough into an elaborate optimization puzzle that requires advanced knowledge of nutritional biochemistry to navigate. Yet the most robust evidence suggests that dietary sufficiency admits far more variation than any specific ideology acknowledges. Populations maintaining excellent health outcomes consume radically different nutritional patterns: Mediterranean populations with high olive oil and moderate wine consumption, Okinawan populations with high vegetable and moderate fish intake, Maasai populations with diets composed primarily of dairy and meat, and Seventh-Day Adventist vegetarians in California. The common elements across healthy dietary patterns include whole foods, minimally processed foods, adequate but not excessive caloric intake, and integration with cultural food traditions that make eating pleasurable rather than stressful. These similarities matter far more than specific macronutrient ratios or food group inclusions, yet receive less attention because they don't support proprietary diet programs or supplement sales.

The diet industry's $72 billion annual revenue depends on maintaining confusion about nutritional sufficiency and generating recurring cycles of insufficiency, intervention, and failure. Commercial weight-loss programs achieve approximately 95% failure rates over five-year periods when success is defined as sustained weight loss of 10% or more, an outcome so consistent that it suggests the interventions address symptoms rather than the causes of weight regulation. Yet rather than questioning the model, the industry frames failure as individual insufficiency: inadequate willpower, insufficient commitment, failure to follow protocols precisely. This deflection obscures the physiological reality that bodies defend set-point weights through powerful regulatory mechanisms. When caloric restriction produces weight loss, metabolic rate decreases, hunger hormones increase, satiety hormones decrease, and energy expenditure from non-exercise activity drops, a coordinated response that opposes further weight loss and promotes regain. Neuroscientist Stephan Guyenet's research on body weight regulation demonstrates that these adaptations can persist for years after weight loss, meaning the person maintaining 30 pounds below their previous set point may experience permanent hunger elevation and metabolic suppression. Their body perpetually signals nutritional insufficiency even when objectively adequate food is consumed, because regulatory systems target the historical set point rather than current weight. This creates a tragic irony: people pursue weight loss to achieve health and well-being, but the sustained effort to maintain that loss often produces worse health outcomes and diminished well-being than would have resulted from accepting their body's defended weight and focusing on health behaviors independent of weight.

Sleep Debt and the Recovered Rest Fallacy

Modern populations chronically underestimate their sleep requirements, normalizing inadequate rest as adult responsibility while simultaneously experiencing epidemic levels of fatigue-related health consequences. The Centers for Disease Control estimates that one-third of American adults routinely sleep fewer than 7 hours nightly, below the minimum threshold for optimal health outcomes. Yet surveys consistently find that people believe they require less sleep than they actually need, reporting feeling adequately rested on six hours while simultaneously consuming stimulants to maintain alertness and experiencing afternoon energy crashes. This disconnect reflects what sleep researcher William Dement termed "sleep debt", an accumulated deficit between actual and required sleep that impairs cognitive function, emotional regulation, immune response, metabolic health, and cellular repair processes. Sleep debt accumulates incrementally; a person sleeping 90 minutes less than they require nightly accrues a whole night's sleep debt each week, progressively degrading function in ways they may not consciously attribute to insufficient rest. More problematically, moderate chronic sleep restriction produces performance impairments equivalent to acute total sleep deprivation, but without the subjective sleepiness that accompanies pulling all-nighters. Research by Hans Van Dongen, restricting subjects to six hours of sleep nightly for two weeks, found that cognitive performance declined to levels equivalent to two nights of total sleep deprivation. Yet, participants subjectively felt only mildly sleepy, unaware that their decision-making, attention, and memory had deteriorated substantially.

The recovery from chronic sleep debt requires far more than a single night of extended sleep. Studies tracking adults after periods of restricted sleep found that three nights of extended sleep recovered only about one-third of accumulated performance deficits, with full recovery requiring one to two weeks of adequate rest. This delayed recovery timeline explains the common experience of feeling exhausted despite sleeping nine hours on the weekend after a week of abbreviated sleep; the two nights of recovery sleep barely begin addressing the accumulated deficit. Yet schedules structured around 40-60-hour workweeks, evening obligations, and early-morning commitments force millions into patterns in which adequate sleep becomes structurally impossible. The person who must wake at 6:00 AM for work commutes, works until 6:00 PM, faces household responsibilities until 9:00 PM, and requires 90 minutes to decompress before sleeping manages perhaps 6.5 hours of sleep nightly, even with optimal discipline. Their fatigue results not from insufficient rest prioritization but from temporal insufficiency, too many obligations compressed into finite time, with sleep functioning as the variable that absorbs the deficit. Recognizing sleep sufficiency, therefore, extends beyond individual sleep hygiene to confronting structural realities about work hours, commute times, and cultural expectations that treat sleep as a wasteful luxury rather than a biological necessity. The person who would require 8.5 hours nightly to function optimally faces a choice: accept persistent fatigue and health consequences, or restructure obligations sufficiently to protect adequate rest, an option that may require sacrificing income, status, or other goods to preserve bodily well-being.

Medical Minimalism and the Treatment Threshold

The expansion of medical diagnosis and treatment into ever more marginal conditions raises urgent questions about therapeutic sufficiency. When does intervention improve health rather than merely converting normal variation into treated disease? Physician Iona Heath argues that modern medicine has shifted from treating pathology that causes suffering to treating statistical abnormalities regardless of subjective health impact. A person with mildly elevated cholesterol who feels entirely well becomes a patient requiring statins; someone with blood pressure readings slightly above population averages receives antihypertensive medication; a child whose activity level exceeds teacher tolerance thresholds is medicated for attention deficit. Each intervention carries costs, side effects, drug interactions, medicalization of identity, and healthcare expenses that may exceed benefits, particularly for marginal cases where absolute risk reduction remains small despite statistically significant treatment effects. When a drug reduces heart attack risk from 2% to 1.5% over ten years, the relative risk reduction of 25% sounds impressive. Still, the absolute benefit means treating 200 patients to prevent one heart attack, leaving 199 patients without benefit, while all 200 face

159

potential side effects and definite costs. Whether this ratio justifies treatment depends on individual risk tolerance, values, and circumstances in ways that population-level guidelines cannot capture.

The concept of "minimally disruptive medicine," proposed by physician Victor Montori, addresses this by focusing on whether treatments align with patients' capacity and priorities. A 78-year-old with multiple chronic conditions may already take eight medications, attend medical appointments monthly, monitor blood sugar three times daily, and follow complex dietary restrictions. Adding another medication or diagnostic procedure may be technically indicated by disease-specific guidelines, but implementing it exceeds the patient's practical capacity to manage their health regimen; their total treatment burden has surpassed sufficiency, even if each intervention appears reasonable in isolation. Montori's framework asks whether proposed interventions fit within the patient's life rather than targeting abnormal measurements, prioritizing functional outcomes and quality of life over biomarker optimization. This approach recognizes that medical sufficiency means adequate treatment to maintain valued functioning rather than maximal treatment of all detectable abnormalities. The person who can walk comfortably, think clearly, strengthen relationships, and pursue meaningful activities has sufficient health regardless of whether their cholesterol, bone density, or inflammatory markers fall within ideal ranges. Focusing on capabilities and subjective well-being rather than biochemical perfection reorients medicine toward genuine health rather than the medicalization of normal human variation.

Somatic Trust and the Recovery of Embodied Knowing

Rebuilding trust in bodily sufficiency requires what might be termed somatic re-education, consciously cultivating awareness of internal signals that contemporary culture has taught us to override or ignore. Contemplative traditions offer practices specifically designed to develop this capacity. Body scanning meditation, for instance, involves systematically directing attention through the body while noting sensations without judgment or intervention. Regular practice increases interoceptive accuracy, and practitioners become better at detecting subtle signals indicating genuine needs versus conditioned responses or psychological cravings. This enhanced awareness allows distinguishing between hunger requiring food and anxiety producing false hunger signals, between fatigue indicating sleep debt and restlessness indicating insufficient movement, between pain signaling injury and discomfort indicating beneficial adaptation. Research by neuroscientist Fadel Zeidan examining the effects of mindfulness on pain perception found that trained practitioners could experience equivalent nociceptive input while reporting significantly less suffering, not because they felt less sensation, but because they could observe pain without catastrophizing or fearing it, reducing the affective component that makes pain intolerable. This capacity to experience bodily sensations without immediately needing to eliminate them proves crucial for recognizing sufficiency, because sufficiency often involves tolerating mild discomfort rather than perpetually seeking perfect comfort.

The intuitive eating framework developed by nutritionists Evelyn Tribole and Elyse Resch applies these principles specifically to food relationships. Rather than following external dietary rules, intuitive eating teaches people to honor hunger cues, respect fullness signals, find satisfaction in eating, and distinguish between physical hunger and emotional eating. Initial research tracking intuitive eaters found lower rates of disordered eating behaviors, reduced anxiety around food, stable weight maintenance, and improved metabolic markers compared to chronic dieters, suggesting that trusting bodily hunger and satiety signals produces better long-term outcomes than overriding them with calculated restriction. This pattern appears across domains: athletes who train according to how they feel rather than rigid schedules show lower injury rates; people who sleep according to how tired they are rather than arbitrary bedtimes report better sleep quality; individuals who modify their activity based on pain rather than pushing through it recover more quickly from injury. The common thread is treating bodily signals as meaningful information that requires a response rather than as obstacles to overcome through discipline. This requires a fundamental shift from viewing the body as an untrustworthy machine requiring external management to recognizing it as an intelligent system that generally maintains equilibrium when provided adequate conditions and protected from genuine threats. The body knows when enough food has been consumed, when enough rest has been accumulated, and when enough movement has occurred for current recovery capacity. The challenge involves creating conditions that allow those signals to register consciously and developing sufficient trust in somatic intelligence to honor them even when they contradict external prescriptions or cultural expectations. Health sufficiency emerges not from optimal measurement parameters but from coherent functioning aligned with individual capacities and circumstances, a state the body can recognize and maintain if we learn to listen.

Chapter 13: Enough in the Workplace: Achieving Work-Life Balance

The modern employment contract contains an invisible clause that previous generations would have found incomprehensible: the expectation that work will colonize consciousness even during non-working hours. A software engineer closes her laptop at six o'clock but continues mentally debugging code while cooking dinner. A project manager spends Sunday afternoon drafting email responses he won't send until Monday morning, maintaining the performance that he respects, while actually violating the boundaries he respects. A teacher grades papers during her daughter's soccer game, physically present but cognitively absent. This phenomenon, which organizational psychologists term "work-related rumination", represents a fundamental shift in how employment consumes human capacity. While previous industrial eras demanded bodily presence during defined hours, contemporary knowledge work extracts cognitive availability across all waking hours, and increasingly during sleep as work anxieties infiltrate dreams. The question of achieving work-life balance has thus become more complex than simple time allocation; it involves negotiating which mental territories remain protected from occupational encroachment, and whether such protection remains even possible within economic structures that reward constant availability and punish boundary maintenance.

Research by Charlotte Fritz at Portland State University, tracking knowledge workers over six months, found that work-related rumination during off-hours correlated more strongly with burnout, sleep disturbance, and relationship strain than did actual working hours. Two employees working identical fifty-hour weeks exhibited dramatically different outcomes based on whether they could psychologically detach during non-working time. The employee who mentally disengaged, who could attend fully to dinner conversation, could read for pleasure without work intrusions, could exercise without strategizing about upcoming meetings, and showed resilience across health and satisfaction measures. The employee who remained cognitively tethered to work despite physical absence exhibited stress markers comparable to those of someone working 70 hours per week. This finding demolishes the assumption that work-life balance requires limiting hours; it reveals that boundary permeability matters more than its location. The professional who "leaves work at work" by completing tasks within office hours but then spends evenings mentally rehearsing presentations and weekends worrying about team dynamics has not actually created separation. Actual disengagement requires what Fritz terms "psychological detachment", the capacity to stop thinking about work-related concerns altogether, to fully inhabit non-work domains without occupational residue contaminating attention.

The Availability Trap and Signal Asymmetry

Contemporary communication technology has created what labor economists call "enforced flexibility," in which workers are expected to be constantly available. At the same time, employers maintain complete flexibility over when they extract that availability. The smartphone sitting on the bedside table represents a permanent potential interruption, the message from a supervisor arriving at ten PM, the client email received Saturday morning, and the Slack notification during vacation. Workers respond to these intrusions for rational reasons: to demonstrate commitment, to protect their position amid employment precarity, and to avoid the accumulated burden of deferred responses. Yet this responsiveness generates a coordination problem that harms all participants. When one team member responds to evening messages, others feel pressure to match that availability. Response time norms ratchet downward across the group until evening and weekend communication becomes standard expectations rather than exceptional circumstances. Leslie Perlow's research at Harvard Business School examining consulting firms found that teams trapped in this dynamic reported it as involuntary; no individual preferred constant availability, but each felt compelled to maintain it because of others' behavior, creating a collective-action problem in which everyone participates in a pattern nobody wants.

The "signal asymmetry" inherent in digital communication exacerbates this dynamic. Sending a message requires minimal effort, thirty seconds to type and dispatch an email, while receiving that message imposes a substantial cognitive burden. The recipient must interrupt their current activity, parse the request, determine urgency, formulate a response, and then attempt to re-engage with whatever they were doing before the interruption. This asymmetry means senders vastly underestimate the disruption they cause, particularly when the same sender issues multiple small requests rather than batching them. Research by Gloria Mark at the University of California, Irvine, tracking information workers through their daily activities, found that recovering from an interruption required an average of 23 minutes, the time needed to regain the cognitive state that existed before the interruption. A supervisor sending three brief messages across an evening imposes not ninety seconds of recipient time but over an hour of fragmented attention, destroyed focus, and effortful re-engagement. Yet the supervisor experiences only the ninety seconds, making the actual cost invisible to the person imposing it. This creates what economists call "negative externality", costs borne by parties not involved in the decision to generate them, except here the externality involves cognitive capacity and temporal autonomy rather than environmental pollution.

Organizations have begun experimenting with "communication norms" designed to reduce expectations of availability and restore temporal boundaries. Some companies implement "email-free Fridays" where internal messages are prohibited. Others establish "core hours" during which communication is expected and "protected time" during which interruptions violate explicit policy. Volkswagen's German division configured email servers to stop routing messages to employee phones during non-working hours, making after-hours communication technically impossible rather than merely discouraged. These interventions demonstrate mixed results. Research evaluating such policies finds that they succeed only when leadership consistently models the behavior and when violations carry actual consequences. When senior managers praise email-free Fridays while continuing to send messages themselves, or when protected time exists nominally but meeting invitations regularly override it without penalty, workers correctly perceive the policy as performative rather than genuine. The underlying challenge involves misalignment between stated organizational values (employee wellbeing, sustainable pace) and actual reward structures (promotion for those demonstrating "commitment" through constant availability, marginalization of those maintaining boundaries). Until organizations restructure incentives to reward temporal boundaries rather than punish them, individual workers face impossible choices between career advancement and cognitive autonomy.

Occupational Identity Fusion and the Blurred Self

Contemporary professional culture, particularly in high-status knowledge work, actively cultivates what psychologists call "identity fusion", the dissolution of boundaries between occupational role and personal identity. The lawyer who introduces herself at social gatherings by saying "I am a litigator" rather than "I work in litigation" reveals this fusion. The entrepreneur who describes sleepless nights and hundred-hour weeks as "passion" rather than exploitation has internalized their work as existential purpose rather than economic exchange. While previous employment eras maintained more apparent separation, you worked at the factory, but you were not the factory; contemporary professional socialization encourages merging self-concept with occupational function. LinkedIn profiles blur this distinction deliberately: they prompt users to articulate personal mission statements indistinguishable from corporate mission statements, to showcase "thought leadership" that serves employer interests while appearing as authentic personal expression, to develop "personal brands" that make the individual's identity dependent on their market positioning.

This fusion serves organizational interests by making workers psychologically available beyond contracted hours without requiring additional compensation. The employee who perceives work as an expression of identity rather than a labor exchange will respond to evening messages not because they're paid to, but because ignoring them would violate their sense of self. They'll work through illness, not from fear of consequences but because not working feels like abandoning part of who they are. Sociologist Arlie Hochschild, studying Silicon Valley culture, documented how companies deliberately foster identity fusion through

167

language that frames employment as family membership, workplace amenities that reduce the need to leave campus, and mission statements that position products as world-changing rather than commercial. Workers at these firms reported difficulty articulating life goals independent of company objectives, describing personal aspirations that replicated corporate talking points. When Hochschild asked engineers about their long-term hopes, responses like "I want to maximize positive impact through scalable technological solutions" showed language patterns indistinguishable from those in company press releases. These individuals had not consciously chosen to subordinate personal identity to corporate identity; instead, through sustained exposure to an organizational culture that blurred these boundaries, the distinction itself had dissolved.

Establishing work-life balance under conditions of identity fusion requires not time management techniques but identity reconstruction, consciously developing self-concept anchored in domains independent of occupational function. This proves psychologically challenging because work often provides elements crucial to identity: competence through skilled performance, status through professional achievement, purpose through contribution to meaningful projects, and community through colleague relationships. Reducing occupational centrality without replacing these elements risks creating an identity vacuum rather than an identity balance. The research on retirement adjustment illuminates this pattern: individuals whose identity centered heavily on occupational role experience significantly higher rates of depression, cognitive decline, and mortality following retirement than those who maintained robust non-work identities throughout their careers. The finding suggests that work-life balance involves not allocating time between domains but distributing identity investment across multiple life spheres so that self-worth and meaning derive from a portfolio rather than a single source.

The Adequacy Threshold and Strategic Underperformance

Conventional career advice assumes continuous performance maximization: consistently exceed expectations, pursue every opportunity for advancement, and demonstrate relentless improvement. Yet this logic inevitably leads to an ever-expanding workload that consumes more time and energy without corresponding increases in compensation or satisfaction. Economist Juliet Schor's analysis of the "work-spend cycle" reveals how career advancement typically generates lifestyle inflation, maintaining constant financial pressure despite rising income. The associate who works sixty hours weekly, earning $75,000, receives a promotion to senior associate working sixty-five hours weekly, earning $95,000, then increases housing costs, childcare expenses, and consumption standards until financial pressure remains identical despite the raise. The result is that advancement produces intensification without liberation, more work delivering more income that funds more expenses that require more work.

Breaking this cycle requires articulating what organizational psychologists call an "adequacy threshold", the career level and income point that provides sufficient security and satisfaction without requiring sacrifice of other life domains. The threshold varies by individual: one person might determine that a senior individual contributor role with a $110,000 salary provides adequate professional accomplishment and financial security; another might set their threshold at middle management and $150,000. The specific number matters less than the act of conscious definition and commitment to defending that threshold against pressure to exceed it. This approach, which might be termed "strategic career sufficiency", means declining some opportunities, accepting being perceived as less ambitious than peers, and potentially sacrificing income and status that further advancement would provide. Research by Amy Wrzesniewski at the Yale School of Management examining workers across industries found that individuals who consciously set adequacy thresholds and defended them reported significantly higher life satisfaction than those pursuing maximum achievement or those who felt trapped in inadequate positions. The adequacy-threshold group had deliberately chosen positions below their capability ceiling, creating what Wrzesniewski terms "sustainable employment", work that provided sufficient rewards while preserving capacity for other life investments.

The concept threatens organizational cultures that extract maximum effort by keeping adequacy perpetually undefined. If workers know precisely what constitutes enough professionally, enough income, enough status, enough achievement, they can resist pressures to sacrifice everything else in pursuit of more. Companies thus benefit from maintaining ambiguity about sufficiency, from cultivating fear that the current position remains precarious, and from suggesting that anyone not pursuing advancement signals inadequate commitment. The employee who announces "I'm satisfied at this level and don't seek promotion" reveals themselves as someone who won't be exploited through advancement incentives, potentially marking them as culturally misaligned in organizations that equate ambition with value. Yet this very resistance to perpetual escalation represents a sophisticated form of resource allocation: recognizing that career capital is one resource among many, and that optimizing career returns while neglecting relational, physical, creative, and community investments produces portfolio imbalance despite professional success.

Temporal Sovereignty and the Attention Economy

The fundamental resource workers exchange for wages has shifted from physical labor to temporal attention, the capacity to direct consciousness toward employer-designated objectives during contracted hours and increasingly beyond them. This shift has profound implications for work-life balance because attention is non-renewable and zero-sum, unlike physical labor. A construction worker who completes an eight-hour shift has expended physical energy that sleep and nutrition replenish for tomorrow's labor. A knowledge worker who spends eight hours in meetings and on email has expended attention that sleep does not fully restore and that compounds across days without adequate recovery periods. Attention operates more like topsoil than like muscle; you can deplete it faster than it regenerates, and chronic depletion reduces future capacity. Neuroscientist Daniel Levitin's research on cognitive load demonstrates that attention-demanding activities produce measurable cortisol elevation, that this stress response requires substantial recovery time, and that insufficient recovery between attention-demanding periods results in cumulative degradation of cognitive performance, emotional regulation, and immune function.

This reality makes temporal sovereignty, control over when and how one deploys attention, the crucial variable in sustainable employment rather than total hours worked. The worker who controls their schedule, who can batch similar tasks to reduce context-switching costs, who can protect periods of uninterrupted focus, and who can choose when to engage with communication and when to defer it,

171

demonstrates dramatically better cognitive performance and well-being than workers with identical job duties but no schedule autonomy. Sociologist Phyllis Moen's research examining white-collar workers found that flexibility over when and where work occurred predicted health outcomes and job satisfaction more strongly than hours worked or objective job demands. Two employees with the same workload exhibited different outcomes based on whether they controlled how that work was structured. This finding explains why remote work during the pandemic produced divergent experiences: those who used flexibility to create protective routines and boundaries reported improved well-being. In contrast, those who experienced increased interruption and loss of structure reported deterioration. The technology enabled either outcome, depending on whether workers possessed autonomy to structure their temporal environment or faced intensified demands from employers exploiting the blurred boundaries remote work created.

Organizations that genuinely support work-life balance thus need to provide not just flexibility but sovereignty, meaningful control over attention allocation rather than merely permission to work at different times. This requires restructuring evaluation systems that currently measure availability rather than output, that reward responsiveness rather than thoughtful deliberation, and that punish temporal boundaries as insufficient commitment. Some companies have experimented with "results-only work environments," where employees are evaluated solely on defined outputs rather than on time invested or availability demonstrated. Studies of these implementations show mixed results: they succeed in cultures that genuinely measure outcomes and fail in cultures where ROWE is adopted nominally, with managers continuing to evaluate based on presence and responsiveness. The deeper challenge involves acknowledging that many knowledge work roles lack clear output metrics, making evaluation inherently subjective and vulnerable to biases that favor visible busyness over actual contribution. Until organizations develop legitimate capacity to assess knowledge work quality independent of time investment, workers who establish firm temporal boundaries risk being perceived as underperforming regardless of their actual contributions.

Life Domain Negotiation and the Myth of Balance

The metaphor of work-life "balance" implies a stable equilibrium achievable through proper calibration, fifty hours to work, fifty hours to personal life, sixty-eight hours to sleep, leaving whatever remains for everything else. This frame misleads by suggesting that balance is a static state rather than a dynamic negotiation that requires constant adjustment as life circumstances change. The professional with young children faces entirely different constraints than the same professional fifteen years later with adolescent kids; the person caring for aging parents cannot maintain boundaries identical to someone with no dependent-care responsibilities; the individual recovering from illness requires different accommodations than someone in robust health. Researchers studying work-family negotiation increasingly describe the challenge as managing "interference" rather than achieving balance, accepting that domains will conflict, and developing strategies for deciding which takes precedence when. This frame acknowledges irreducible tensions rather than promising harmony through better optimization.

Boundary theory, developed by organizational psychologist Blake Ashforth, distinguishes between "segmentation" strategies that create thick boundaries between life domains and "integration" strategies that allow permeable boundaries. Neither approach proves universally superior; effectiveness depends on personality, occupation type, and life circumstances. Some individuals thrive when work and personal life remain completely separate; they change clothes upon arriving home, maintain separate phones for work and personal communication, and refuse to discuss work during personal time. Others prefer integration; they'll answer work emails while watching children's sporting events, but also handle personal errands during work hours, discuss work challenges with partners, and bring family photos to the office. They see artificial separation as more stressful than flexible blending. Research by Ellen Kossek at Purdue University found that alignment between preferred boundary strategy and actual boundary permeability predicted well-being better than any particular strategy type. This person prefers segmentation but faces organizational demands for integration, which causes chronic stress due to violated boundaries. Similarly, the person who prefers integration but works in a culture demanding strict separation feels constrained by artificial divisions.

The recognition that optimal strategies vary from person to person has implications for organizational policy: one-size-fits-all approaches to work-life balance inevitably suit some workers while disadvantaging others. Flexible work arrangements, compressed schedules, unlimited vacation policies, and remote work options provide helpful tools only when workers have genuine autonomy to use them according to their actual needs, rather than having to follow utilization patterns that signal appropriate commitment to managers. Multiple studies document that workers, particularly women and marginalized groups, underutilize flexibility policies due to fear that doing so marks them as less severe professionals. The policy exists nominally, but organizational culture punishes use through subtle status penalties, assignment of less desirable projects, and exclusion from opportunities. Until organizations address the reward structures that create these penalties, providing flexibility tools without cultural transformation merely adds to the performance burden; workers must now navigate complex decisions about when the use of flexibility will be perceived as a reasonable accommodation versus inadequate dedication.

The key question is whether traditional employment structures, built for manufacturing, can adapt to knowledge work that values mental clarity over hours worked. Industrial production increased efficiency by intensifying labor and using better techniques and machines to boost hourly output. Knowledge work cannot be similarly intensified; you cannot think twice as many valuable thoughts per hour through better technique. Yet organizational management continues to apply industrial logic to cognitive labor, measuring inputs rather than outputs and assuming that more hours produce better results. Substantial evidence suggests the opposite: research across multiple knowledge work domains finds that productivity peaks around forty-five to fifty weekly hours and declines substantially beyond that threshold as cognitive depletion outweighs additional time invested. The software engineer working 70 hours weekly produces not 40% more code than one working 50 hours, but substantially less code of lower quality, with more defects requiring later remediation. Yet companies continue to demand extended hours because they lack frameworks for evaluating the quality of cognitive work independent of visible effort.

Creating genuine workplace sufficiency will require more than individual boundary-setting or corporate wellness programs; it demands reconceptualizing employment relationships to acknowledge that cognitive labor operates under constraints different from those of physical production. This might involve compensating knowledge workers for cognitive capacity deployed rather than hours worked, structuring projects around sustainable cognitive load rather than deadline pressure, and accepting that knowledge quality requires protected recovery time rather than constant availability. Whether organizations will make these adjustments voluntarily or require regulatory intervention remains uncertain. What is certain is that current arrangements produce unsustainable cognitive extraction that diminishes both worker wellbeing and, paradoxically, the quality of work organizations receive. Establishing enough in the workplace requires recognizing that human attention is a finite resource requiring careful stewardship rather than an infinite well from which employers can extract perpetually without consequence.

Chapter 14: Financial Independence: Redefining Wealth

The conventional pathway to financial independence follows a predictable architecture: accumulate sufficient investment capital to generate passive income exceeding living expenses, thereby liberating oneself from the necessity of employment. Financial independence communities frame this objective through the "4% rule", the principle that a portfolio can sustain annual withdrawals of 4% indefinitely without depleting principal. This means someone requiring $40,000 annually needs a $1,000,000 portfolio to achieve independence. This mathematical clarity creates seductive simplicity: financial freedom reduces to a calculable number, and reaching that number solves the problem of economic security permanently. Yet this formulation contains assumptions so fundamental they become invisible, assumptions about what constitutes security, what independence actually means, and whether the relationship between wealth and freedom operates as straightforwardly as multiplication tables suggest. The person who reaches their financial independence number often discovers an unexpected phenomenon: the goal that promised liberation frequently generates new forms of anxiety. Will the portfolio withstand the subsequent market correction? Should withdrawals be reduced to preserve capital longer? What if inflation exceeds projections? The target that appeared to represent "enough" reveals itself as arbitrary, and the fundamental question, how much wealth is genuinely sufficient?, remains unanswered even after achieving the supposed answer.

This paradox arises because the discourse on financial independence confuses means with ends. Money functions as an instrumental good, valuable for what it enables rather than intrinsically. Focusing on simply accumulating wealth turns money into an end in itself, rather than a means to an end. Philosopher Georg Simmel noted that in modern capitalism, people often pursue such goods for their own sake, losing sight of their original purposes. The person accumulating toward financial independence may find, upon reaching the threshold, that they never clearly articulated what they wanted independence *for*, which activities would fill liberated time, which relationships would receive attention previously claimed by employment, and which latent capacities would finally receive development. Without clarity about independence's purpose, the achievement provides only negative freedom (freedom *from* employment necessity) without corresponding positive freedom (freedom *to* pursue specific meaningful activities). This deficit creates a vacuum that anxiety rushes to fill, as individuals realize that eliminating one constraint does not automatically reveal what should replace it.

The Illusion of Portfolio Permanence

The mathematical models underpinning financial independence calculations are based on historical market returns spanning roughly a century of American economic history, a period characterized by exceptional circumstances that may not replicate. The United States emerged from World War II as the dominant global economy with an intact industrial infrastructure while competitor nations rebuilt from devastation, creating asymmetric advantages that fueled decades of extraordinary returns. The 4% withdrawal rule derives from research by financial planner William Bengen analyzing historical portfolio performance from 1926-1992, finding that a 60% stock/40% bond portfolio could sustain 4% inflation-adjusted annual withdrawals for at least thirty years across all historical starting points in that dataset. Yet this backward-looking analysis cannot account for structural changes that may render historical patterns unreliable: demographic shifts as populations age and retiree-to-worker ratios increase, climate disruptions that may fundamentally alter economic productivity, technological displacement that might concentrate returns among narrow capital holders while eliminating broad employment, or geopolitical reconfigurations as American economic dominance wanes. Financial advisor Michael Kitces has documented that sequence-of-returns risk, the risk that poor market performance early in retirement depletes portfolios before recovery, makes the 4% rule considerably more fragile than commonly assumed. A retiree beginning withdrawals just before a significant market decline may find their portfolio unsustainable even if average returns over their lifetime would theoretically support withdrawals, because selling depreciated assets to fund living expenses locks in losses that prevent participation in subsequent recovery.

Beyond sequence risk lies the more fundamental question of whether financial markets can maintain historical return patterns in a world confronting ecological limits and resource constraints. Conventional investment returns depend on economic growth, which historically has correlated with rising energy and material consumption. If ecological boundaries require wealthy economies to reduce material throughput, as planetary boundaries research suggests, then sustained market returns comparable to those of the twentieth century become questionable. Economist Tim Jackson's study, which models economic growth under carbon constraints, demonstrates that maintaining GDP growth while reducing emissions to sustainable levels requires decoupling economic output from energy consumption at rates never achieved historically and likely physically impossible given thermodynamic constraints. If economic growth stagnates or contracts in wealthy nations, the investment returns that financial independence calculations assume may not materialize, leaving individuals who structured their lives around portfolio-income projections economically vulnerable despite having "saved enough" by conventional standards. This possibility reveals how deeply financial independence strategies embed assumptions about the continuation of specific historical conditions, assumptions that current trajectories increasingly call into question.

The Hidden Infrastructure of Independence

Financial independence discussions typically focus on portfolio size while treating the infrastructure enabling that portfolio's utility as given and stable. Yet the capacity of accumulated wealth to provide security depends entirely on functioning systems that individuals cannot personally control: legal frameworks protecting property rights and enforcing contracts, financial institutions maintaining account records and facilitating transactions, currency stability preserving purchasing power, supply chains delivering goods and services that money purchases, and social stability preventing violence or expropriation. These infrastructure layers, legal, financial, monetary, logistical, and social, constitute the actual foundation upon which financial independence rests. Yet, they receive minimal attention in independence planning because they appear so stable as to be permanent. Historical perspective reveals this assumption as fragile. Multiple twentieth-century examples demonstrate how quickly savings can lose value through currency collapse (Weimar Germany, Zimbabwe, Venezuela), how property rights can be retroactively nullified (postwar asset confiscations, nationalization programs), how financial system failures can make wealth inaccessible (bank runs, frozen accounts during crises), and how social breakdown can render monetary wealth irrelevant when goods become unavailable at any price.

This infrastructure dependence means that financial independence, as conventionally conceived, represents at best interdependence, reliance on complex social systems rather than on specific employers. True freedom would require not merely accumulated capital but actual productive capacity: land producing food, skills generating value, social networks providing reciprocal support, and knowledge enabling adaptation to changing circumstances. The difference between these forms of security became vivid during the COVID-19 pandemic disruptions, when supply chain breakdowns made certain goods unavailable regardless of purchasing power, when medical systems became overwhelmed, making wealth insufficient to guarantee treatment access, and when social isolation revealed that accumulated money could not substitute for community relationships. These disruptions highlighted what Indigenous land-based communities have long understood: genuine security derives not from abstracted monetary stores but from embedded relationships, with ecosystems providing sustenance, with communities providing mutual aid, and with place-specific knowledge enabling resilience. Financial wealth is one potential component of security, but treating it as synonymous with security itself is a category error that becomes apparent during systemic disruptions, when abstract wealth cannot easily be converted into concrete needs. The person with a million-dollar portfolio but no practical skills, no community ties, no local ecological knowledge, and no capacity for self-provisioning may discover during a crisis that their independence was largely illusory, dependent on the stability of the very systems they imagined they had escaped.

Redefining Wealth Through Non-Market Capital

Academic research on wealth is increasingly recognizing forms of capital that conventional financial accounting ignores. Sociologist Pierre Bourdieu's analysis identified cultural capital (knowledge, skills, education, cultural competencies), social capital (relationships, networks, community connections), and symbolic capital (reputation, honor, prestige) as forms of wealth that function distinctively from economic capital but can be converted under specific circumstances. Someone with extensive social capital may access opportunities, information, or assistance that money alone could not purchase; someone with substantial cultural capital may generate economic returns through expertise that exceeds their financial assets. More recently, ecological economist Robert Costanza and colleagues have attempted to quantify natural capital, the value of ecosystem services like water purification, climate regulation, pollination, and nutrient cycling that enable economic activity but appear on no balance sheet. Their controversial estimates value global ecosystem services at roughly twice global GDP annually, suggesting that the natural capital underpinning economic systems vastly exceeds the financial capital we meticulously track and accumulate. This research challenges the assumption that monetary wealth accurately represents total wealth or that maximizing financial assets necessarily optimizes overall security and well-being.

Anthropological studies of non-market economies reveal alternative wealth conceptions that prioritize different forms of accumulation. In many gift economy societies, wealth manifests not as stored goods but as social obligations, the number of people who owe you reciprocal support because you previously assisted them. The "wealthy" person in such systems is one with extensive networks of mutual obligation, making them resource-poor by conventional standards but support-rich when needs arise. Anthropologist David Graeber's research documented how systems of mutual credit, tracking who owes what to whom across communities, functioned for millennia as economic infrastructure without requiring monetary accumulation or formal financial institutions. These alternative systems suggest that wealth fundamentally represents a claim on resources or capacities rather than the possession of abstract monetary units. A person with deep community integration, diverse practical skills, ecological knowledge enabling food production, strong health supporting physical capacity, and extensive social networks providing mutual aid possesses genuine wealth despite potentially minimal financial assets. Conversely, the financially wealthy person lacking these alternative capitals may find their ostensible wealth fragile, unable to easily convert financial assets into actual security or well-being when social or ecological systems experience stress.

This expanded understanding of wealth suggests that financial independence strategies that focus exclusively on investment portfolio accumulation systematically underinvest in alternative capital that might provide more robust security. Time spent earning additional income to maximize savings rate is time not spent building community relationships, developing practical skills, cultivating reciprocal support networks, or deepening place-based knowledge. The person who retires at forty with a million-dollar portfolio but no friends, no practical capacities, no community connections, and no sense of purpose faces a qualitatively different situation than someone who retires at fifty-five with a smaller portfolio but extensive social integration, diverse competencies, and a clear sense of meaning and contribution. Which individual has achieved genuine independence remains unclear, yet the discourse on financial independence consistently privileges the former while largely ignoring the latter's alternative wealth forms. This blind spot reflects how thoroughly modern consciousness has internalized market logic, treating only monetized value as real wealth while rendering invisible the multiple forms of capital that enable actual human flourishing and resilience.

The Temporal Trap of Delayed Living

The journey toward financial independence typically requires substantial sacrifice of present consumption to enable future freedom, working jobs that may feel meaningless, postponing experiences or relationships that the current life stage makes available, tolerating living conditions below what income could support, and structuring daily existence around accumulation rather than immediate satisfaction. This intertemporal trade-off assumes that future freedom will be valuable enough to justify the present constraint and that the person who reaches financial independence will retain the capacity, desire, and circumstances to use that freedom meaningfully. Yet these assumptions prove less reliable than financial independence planning acknowledges. Research on affective forecasting, already covered in previous chapters, demonstrates systematic errors in predicting future preferences. Still, temporal discounting research reveals additional complications: we dramatically undervalue our present experience relative to imagined futures, yet when those futures arrive, we discover we have not escaped our present selves but rather carried them forward. The person who spent fifteen years working intensively to reach financial independence at forty may discover at forty that they have habituated to work-intensive lifestyle, that their identity has organized around career achievement, that their relationships have atrophied during accumulation years, and that they lack clear sense of how to structure liberated time because they have spent their thirties, the period when many identity-defining interests and relationships form, focused on economic accumulation rather than personal development.

The implicit assumption underlying delayed gratification is that life divides into distinct phases: the accumulation phase, which requires sacrifice, and the independence phase, which enables fulfillment. Yet lived experience reveals greater continuity: habits, relationships, capacities, and orientations developed over the accumulation years tend to persist rather than magically transform upon reaching financial milestones. The person who defers travel until retirement may find that physical capacity for adventure travel has declined, that travel companions are no longer available as friends have scattered or are constrained by their own work obligations, or that their tolerance for discomfort and novelty has diminished after decades of routine. The individual who postpones creative pursuits until achieving financial freedom may discover that the neuroplasticity that enables skill acquisition operates more robustly in younger decades, that creative communities have formed around others who consistently participate rather than wait for economic security, or that the mental space creativity requires has been colonized by financial monitoring and portfolio management. These patterns suggest that aggressive financial independence pursuit may involve hidden costs that only become apparent when the delayed future finally arrives, revealing that freedom purchased through years of deferral is qualitatively different from freedom integrated throughout life stages when specific capacities and opportunities were available.

Sufficiency-Based Financial Security Versus Independence Maximization

An alternative approach to financial security involves identifying sufficiency thresholds rather than pursuing independence maximization. This reframing asks not "How much do I need never to work again?" but rather "What level of financial reserve provides adequate security while permitting present-oriented living?" Sufficiency-based financial planning recognizes that perfect security is impossible, unforeseen medical needs, economic disruptions, or longevity exceeding projections can overwhelm any reserve, but that incremental security gains beyond certain thresholds provide diminishing returns while consuming ever-increasing present sacrifice. Research by Daniel Kahneman and Angus Deaton examining income and wellbeing in the United States found that emotional wellbeing improved with income up to approximately $75,000 annually (in 2010 dollars), beyond which further income increases showed minimal wellbeing gains. While this research examines income rather than accumulated wealth, it suggests thresholds at which additional financial resources yield marginal rather than transformative improvements. A sufficiency approach would identify adequate reserves, perhaps six months to two years of living expenses for employment disruption, adequate healthcare coverage for medical emergencies, and modest retirement savings to supplement social insurance programs, then prioritize present-oriented living rather than maximum accumulation.

This approach contradicts financial independence orthodoxy by accepting ongoing employment or income-generating activity as potentially sustainable and even desirable rather than as a constraint requiring escape. The reframing asks what work would feel sufficient, meaningful enough to sustain indefinitely, compensated adequately to meet needs, demanding reasonable rather than excessive hours, and compatible with other valued activities, rather than assuming all employment constitutes undesirable necessity to be minimized. Sociological research on work satisfaction reveals that autonomy, competence, relatedness, and meaningful contribution predict satisfaction far more reliably than compensation level or hours worked. Someone working 30 hours per week in meaningful activity with substantial autonomy and a clear sense of contribution may experience their work as enriching rather than depleting, making the drive to accumulate sufficient capital to eliminate work less compelling. Under sufficiency-based financial security, the goal is not to escape work but to achieve financial stability that enables choosing meaningful work unconstrained by immediate economic desperation. This might involve building reserves sufficient to cover employment gaps while seeking better positions, refusing exploitative conditions, supporting periods of retraining or education, or permitting reduced hours, trading income for time. The focus shifts from achieving permanent work elimination to gaining negotiating position and flexibility, a more modest yet potentially more achievable and satisfying objective than complete financial independence.

Sufficiency approaches also recognize that security needs evolve across life stages rather than remaining static. The financial reserves adequate for a healthy thirty-five-year-old differ substantially from those appropriate for a sixty-five-year-old confronting age-related medical needs and approaching end-of-life planning. Rather than targeting a single financial independence number calculated in young adulthood and pursued relentlessly for decades, sufficiency planning involves periodic reassessment: do current reserves provide adequate security for present life circumstances?

What emerging risks or opportunities does the present life stage present? What adjustments would enhance security without requiring radical sacrifice? This ongoing calibration prevents the trap of endlessly pursuing ever-larger targets because the goalposts keep receding, and it maintains a connection between financial strategy and actual lived experience rather than treating accumulation as an autonomous objective disconnected from specific purposes it supposedly serves. The person who reaches what they previously defined as their sufficiency threshold can choose to continue accumulating if that process proves meaningful, or can redirect energy toward non-financial pursuits if adequate security has been achieved, maintaining optionality rather than being locked into a predetermined trajectory.

Wealth as Relationship Rather Than Possession

Perhaps the most fundamental redefinition of wealth involves reconceptualizing it not as something one possesses but as a particular type of relationship to resources, time, and possibility. In this framing, wealth manifests not in account balances but in states of being: sufficiency consciousness that recognizes and appreciates adequacy; autonomy in choosing how to allocate time and attention; capacity to act generously without calculation; freedom from anxiety about scarcity; and authority to decline opportunities or relationships that drain rather than nourish. These qualities can emerge across a wide range of financial circumstances and are largely independent of absolute asset levels. Someone earning a modest income but living well below their means, with minimal fixed obligations, strong social support networks, diverse practical skills, and a clear sense of purpose, may experience themselves as wealthy in these deeper senses despite limited financial assets. Conversely, someone with millions in investments but a lifestyle inflation-matching income, weak relationships, limited practical capacities, anxiety about maintaining wealth, and no clear sense of purpose beyond accumulation may experience themselves as perpetually insufficient despite ostensible wealth.

This relational understanding of wealth suggests that the pathway to financial independence, as commonly conceived, maximizing accumulation through intensive employment and deferred consumption, may actually move people away from genuine wealth if it degrades relationships, diminishes present experience, generates anxiety, and narrows life to monetary dimensions. True financial freedom might require not escaping work but instead finding sufficiently meaningful and manageable work; not maximizing portfolio size but rather calibrating reserves to provide adequate security without consuming all energy in pursuit; not deferring satisfaction until some future milestone but rather integrating sufficient present enjoyment that life feels adequate at each stage rather than perpetually preparatory. From this perspective, wealth redefinition involves expansion rather than substitution, recognizing financial security as one element within a larger constellation of factors contributing to life adequacy rather than treating monetary accumulation as a sufficient condition for freedom. The financially independent person who lacks community, meaning, health, relationships, or purpose has achieved something, certainly, but whether they have gained wealth in any sense that matters remains far from obvious. The work of redefining wealth, then, involves the challenging process of articulating what constitutes genuine sufficiency in one's particular life, resisting cultural messages that conflate wealth with financial assets exclusively, and having the courage to structure financial life around those authentic sufficiency definitions even when they contradict conventional financial independence orthodoxy.

Chapter 15: The Journey to Personal Fulfillment and Satisfaction

Personal fulfillment operates as a recursive phenomenon, a state that simultaneously results from and generates the very conditions that sustain it. Unlike achievement-based satisfaction, which arrives and departs in discrete episodes tied to specific accomplishments, fulfillment functions as a continuous orientation toward existence that persists across changing circumstances. The fulfilled person experiences setbacks, disappointments, and losses without a fundamental disruption of their underlying sense that life, as currently configured, possesses inherent worth. This quality distinguishes fulfillment from happiness, contentment, or pleasure, states we explored in earlier chapters through different lenses. Fulfillment represents something more fundamental: the felt experience that one's existence is justified not by what it produces or achieves but by what it is. Philosopher Susan Wolf, in her work "Meaning in Life and Why It Matters," identifies this distinction through what she terms "active engagement with projects of worth." Fulfillment emerges not from passive reception of pleasant experiences or from achievement of socially validated milestones, but from ongoing participation in activities that one's deepest evaluative faculties recognize as genuinely valuable. This formulation helps explain why pursuing fulfillment proves so difficult; it arises as a byproduct of living according to principles one cannot fully articulate until one has already embodied them. The journey to fulfillment, therefore, resembles less a navigation toward a fixed destination and more a process of discovering what one has, all along, been journeying toward.

The architecture of personal fulfillment rests on what developmental psychologists call "eudaimonic orientation", the capacity to evaluate life not by hedonic tone (whether experiences feel pleasant) but by coherence between action and authenticity. Research by psychologist Veronika Huta at the University of Ottawa, tracking individuals across multiple decades, found that those who scored high on eudaimonic measures, pursuing activities aligned with personal values even when difficult or unrewarding in conventional terms, demonstrated remarkable stability in life satisfaction across circumstances that dramatically disrupted the well-being of more hedonically-oriented individuals. Job loss, relationship dissolution, and health challenges that would devastate someone whose fulfillment depended on specific outcomes produced manageable perturbations for eudaimonically-oriented individuals, who experienced these events as plot developments in ongoing narratives rather than catastrophic failures invalidating their existence. This resilience stems from fulfillment's independence from external validation or circumstantial stability. The person whose sense of life's worthiness depends on maintaining specific conditions, employment status, relationship configuration, health parameters, and financial position has outsourced their existential security to factors beyond their control. The eudaimonically fulfilled person has internalized their evaluative ground, asking not "Are circumstances favorable?" but rather "Am I responding to circumstances in ways that express my deepest commitments?" This internal locus makes fulfillment paradoxically more stable than security-based approaches that attempt to eliminate uncertainty through control.

The Sufficiency Spiral and Iterative Satisfaction

Personal fulfillment develops through what we might term a "sufficiency spiral", a self-reinforcing cycle in which recognizing adequacy in one domain enhances perceptions of sufficiency across other areas, which in turn deepens the original recognition. This mechanism operates differently from the hedonic treadmill or the gratitude practices examined earlier. Where the treadmill involves adaptation that neutralizes satisfaction, and gratitude involves conscious redirection of attention, the sufficiency spiral describes an organic process through which lived experience of enough in specific instances gradually reshapes one's entire evaluative framework. A person who discovers that cooking simple meals from basic ingredients provides as much satisfaction as elaborate restaurant experiences doesn't merely save money; they fundamentally recalibrate their understanding of what constitutes adequate nourishment. This recalibration then influences how they approach other domains: if culinary satisfaction doesn't require gourmet complexity, perhaps entertainment doesn't require premium streaming services; perhaps exercise doesn't require a gym membership; perhaps professional identity doesn't require constant advancement. Each recognition of sufficiency in a specific domain provides evidence challenging the scarcity assumption governing other areas.

Research by positive psychologist Todd Kashdan at George Mason University, examining what he calls "psychological flexibility," reveals how this spiral operates at the neurological level. Participants who successfully reduced consumption in one area, say, deliberate wardrobe simplification, showed increased activity in the ventromedial prefrontal cortex during decision-making tasks in completely unrelated domains, such as financial planning or time management. This brain region integrates emotional information with cognitive evaluation to guide choices, and its enhanced activity suggested that the experience of sufficiency in one area was being generalized as a decision-making heuristic across contexts. The participants weren't consciously applying lessons from closet organization to investment strategy; rather, the embodied experience of "less proving adequate" was reshaping their unconscious evaluative processes. This finding has profound implications for understanding the development of fulfillment: it suggests that fulfillment cannot be achieved through the top-down implementation of a comprehensive life philosophy. Instead, it emerges bottom-up through accumulated experiences of sufficiency that gradually consolidate into a generalized orientation. The journey to fulfillment, therefore, necessarily involves experimentation, testing boundaries of enough in low-stakes domains to generate evidence that challenges scarcity assumptions, allowing that evidence to percolate through cognitive and emotional systems, and gradually expanding sufficient-focused living into domains that previously seemed to require maximization.

The sufficiency spiral also operates temporally, reshaping how individuals relate to their own histories. Psychologist Dan McAdams at Northwestern University, studying life narrative construction, identifies that fulfilled individuals characteristically reinterpret past experiences, including painful ones, as integral to their current selves rather than as detours or failures to be overcome. Where someone oriented toward achievement-based satisfaction might view a failed business venture as wasted years only redeemed by subsequent success, the fulfilled person integrates that experience as an essential developmental chapter that shaped capacities they now value. This reinterpretation doesn't minimize difficulty or romanticize struggle. Instead, it recognizes that one's current self, the self one finds worth inhabiting, emerged from the totality of lived experience, including its difficulties. McAdams terms this "narrative redemption," though the label slightly mischaracterizes the process: the past isn't being redeemed by the present so much as revealed as already sufficient to have produced the present. This temporal sufficiency, the recognition that one's history, with all its detours and apparent inefficiencies, was adequate to generate one's current existence, provides a form of existential closure. The person ceases asking "What should I have done differently?" and begins asking "Given that this history produced me, what does that suggest about who I am and might become?" This shift from counterfactual regret to actual inheritance fundamentally alters one's relationship to time, replacing scarcity of "not enough years to become who I should be" with sufficiency of "enough time elapsed to become someone worth being."

Relational Depth and the Intimacy Economy

Personal fulfillment proves impossible to achieve or sustain in isolation, a reality that distinguishes it from happiness, which can be experienced solitarily through pleasant circumstances or internal states. Fulfillment requires what philosopher Martin Buber termed "I-Thou" encounters, moments when another person is experienced not as an object (I-It) to be utilized or managed but as a subject with their own irreducible interiority. Research by social psychologist Arthur Aron examining the conditions that generate intimacy found that the critical variable wasn't the duration of acquaintance, similarity of interests, or frequency of interaction, but rather the degree to which interactions involved mutual self-disclosure of authentic emotional experience. Aron's famous "36 Questions" study demonstrated that strangers engaging in progressive mutual vulnerability for less than an hour reported feeling closer to each other than to acquaintances they'd known for months. This finding reveals something crucial about fulfillment's relational dimension: it doesn't require extensive social networks or numerous friendships, but instead encounters of sufficient depth in which one feels genuinely known and simultaneously recognizes the other as genuinely knowable.

This insight challenges common assumptions about relational fulfillment requiring either romantic partnership or extensive friend groups. Many deeply fulfilled individuals maintain small relational circles but experience those relationships as fully adequate precisely because their quality admits nothing lacking. The concept of "enough" in relationships thus depends not on quantity but on what we might call "relational depth-to-breadth ratio." A person with three friendships characterized by complete psychological safety, mutual knowledge encompassing each person's evolving values and struggles, and sustained availability during crisis possesses greater relational wealth than someone with thirty acquaintances with whom they cannot be authentic. The fulfilled person has typically discovered this through what social researcher Brené Brown calls "vulnerability winnowing", the process of testing which relationships can sustain authentic self-disclosure and gradually investing more deeply in those that can, while allowing more superficial connections to attenuate naturally. This winnowing appears harsh when described abstractly, but proves liberating in practice: it represents ceasing to perform inauthentic versions of oneself for audiences who never desired those performances. The relief of being known, really known, with one's uncertainties and insufficiencies visible, by even a few people who remain present, creates a foundation that makes fulfillment possible. Without such relationships, individuals experience what sociologist Robert Putnam calls "bowling alone", functioning adequately across life domains while feeling fundamentally unseen, unwitnessed, and existentially solitary.

The "intimacy economy" describes how relational depth requires resource investments that compete with other demands. Unlike financial economies where wealth can be accumulated through others' labor, intimacy requires personal presence that cannot be outsourced. The executive who can delegate professional tasks, hire household management, purchase meal preparation, and automate administrative functions cannot similarly delegate the vulnerability and attentiveness that generate relational depth. Research by sociologist Arlie Hochschild on "time binds" in dual-career couples reveals that even when partners explicitly prioritize their relationship, the cognitive and emotional energy required for authentic intimacy becomes unavailable after days spent in roles that demand professional competence. Partners become intimacy-depleted, capable of coordinating logistics and discussing children, but unable to access the emotional presence required for encounters that actually nourish. This depletion creates a cruel irony: people work extended hours partly to provide for their families, but the working itself consumes the resource, authentic presence, that families most require. Fulfillment in such circumstances becomes structurally precluded not by insufficient time per se but by insufficient cognitive and emotional bandwidth remaining after other domains extract their requirements. The journey to fulfillment, therefore, necessarily involves examining how one's life architecture either permits or prevents the relational presence that fulfillment depends upon, then making potentially uncomfortable structural adjustments that create space for depth. This may mean reduced work hours, declined social obligations, eliminated commitments, or relocated residence to live nearer to key relationships, changes that contradict achievement-oriented advice about maximizing opportunities and maintaining extensive networks.

Purposeful Limitation and the Freedom of Constraint

Counterintuitively, fulfillment often intensifies through deliberate limitation rather than through the expansion of options. This paradox appears across domains: artists working within strict formal constraints usually produce more innovative work than when given complete creative freedom; athletes who specialize in one sport typically achieve higher mastery and satisfaction than multi-sport generalists; scholars who narrow research focus generate more significant contributions than those maintaining broad but shallow expertise across multiple areas. Psychologist Barry Schwartz's research on "the tyranny of choice" demonstrates that decision satisfaction correlates negatively with options beyond approximately six alternatives; more choices generate anxiety and decreased satisfaction regardless of which option is ultimately selected. While we examined choice overload earlier in our discussion of digital information, the principle applies more broadly to life architecture: the person attempting to simultaneously optimize career achievement, relationship depth, physical fitness, creative expression, community involvement, continuous learning, and financial independence typically achieves mediocrity across all domains while experiencing persistent inadequacy. The paradox is that limitation generates fulfillment, not despite but because of the reduced optionality it imposes.

This mechanism operates through what anthropologist David Graeber termed "the elimination of infinite regress." When all options remain perpetually available, every choice implicitly denies all alternative possibilities, creating a cognitive burden of perpetual justification for why this option rather than that one. The person who maintains career optionality by avoiding specialization can never fully invest in their current role because doing so forecloses alternatives they've worked to preserve. The person who keeps multiple romantic possibilities "on deck" can never fully commit to a partner because doing so eliminates options that their lifestyle has been structured to maintain. By contrast, the person who deliberately eliminates options through irreversible commitments, accepting a position that precludes specific career paths, marrying someone who removes other relational possibilities, and having children, which eliminates particular lifestyle options, paradoxically experiences greater freedom because the decision burden has been resolved. They can now ask "Given these commitments, what's possible?" rather than being paralyzed by "What should I commit to?" Fulfillment researcher Emily Esfahani Smith found that individuals reporting the highest life satisfaction typically described themselves as having made "irrevocable commitments" to specific people, places, or projects, precisely the kind of limitation that option-preservation culture treats as a dangerous constraint.

The concept of "productive constraint" appears in creativity research but extends to fulfillment more broadly. Composer Igor Stravinsky claimed that "the more constraints one imposes, the more one frees oneself." This seeming contradiction resolves when we recognize that constraints eliminate decision paralysis and channel energy toward depth within bounded domains. The novelist who commits to a specific character and setting can explore that territory comprehensively; the novelist who constantly reconsiders whether different characters or settings might be more interesting never achieves depth anywhere. Research by organizational psychologist Teresa Amabile, examining creative productivity, found that "intrinsic constraints", limitations that creators impose on themselves as enabling structures, enhanced both output quality and creator satisfaction, while "extrinsic constraints", restrictions imposed by others or circumstances, tended to inhibit both. This distinction matters because it suggests that fulfillment requires not eliminating all constraints but deliberately choosing which constraints to keep. The fulfilled person isn't unconstrained but somewhat constrained by commitments they've consciously selected as worthy of limiting their options. The parent who experiences childcare responsibilities as oppressive constraints likely feels trapped by circumstances; the parent who recognizes childcare as a chosen commitment structuring their life feels engaged with something they've deliberately prioritized. The external situation is identical; the fulfillment diverges based on whether the limitation is experienced as an imposed burden or a chosen architecture.

Temporal Sufficiency and the Resolution of Becoming

Personal fulfillment requires achieving what we might call "temporal sufficiency", the sense that one's allocation of finite lifetime has been adequate to the task of becoming someone worth having been. This differs from conventional productivity or achievement by focusing not on output but on developmental coherence: Has enough time been devoted to becoming the particular configuration of capacities, sensibilities, and commitments that currently constitute my self? Developmental psychologist Erik Erikson's concept of "ego integrity", the final stage in his psychosocial development model, captures this recognition: the person who achieves integrity experiences their life as a coherent whole, while those who don't experience "despair" at unrealized possibilities and inadequate self-becoming. Erikson's model has been challenged for its rigid stage structure, but his core insight about the importance of existential coherence remains valid. Research by gerontologist Robert Butler examining end-of-life psychological states found that individuals reporting life satisfaction in their final years weren't necessarily those who achieved conventional success markers, but rather those who could construct coherent narratives explaining how their lived experiences shaped their current selves. The person who became a teacher rather than pursuing the originally planned medical career finds fulfillment not by minimizing this deviation but by articulating how teaching expresses values they discovered through the very process of deviating from their plan.

This retrospective coherence creates a particular relationship to time that differs markedly from future-oriented goal pursuit. Goal-oriented individuals experience present moments as instrumental, valuable primarily as means to desired futures. The runner logging training miles isn't present at today's run but instead is focused on next month's race; the investor reviewing portfolios isn't engaged with the current financial configuration but instead is projecting decades ahead toward retirement. This future-focus creates what philosopher Martin Heidegger termed "inauthentic temporality", living primarily in anticipation of what's not yet real while treating what is real as a mere transitional stage. By contrast, temporally sufficient individuals experience present moments as intrinsically complete, not because nothing remains to become, but because current activity expresses ongoing commitment rather than incomplete preparation. The runner who is fulfilled runs today not primarily to enable future performance but because running expresses their present identity; future races may occur, but today's run possesses inherent rather than merely instrumental value. This shift doesn't eliminate planning or goal-pursuit but subordinates them: goals serve present identity rather than present activity serving future goals.

The concept of "narrative closure" describes how fulfilled individuals relate to their personal histories. Psychologist

Dan McAdams has documented that fulfilled individuals characteristically tell life stories with coherent themes connecting past, present, and anticipated future into unified arcs, even when external events appear discontinuous or contradictory. Someone who changes careers, relocates repeatedly, or experiences relationship transitions might seem to lack coherence from an external view. Still, if they can articulate the values or commitments that persisted across these changes, they experience their history as unified. This narrative capacity isn't about self-deception or rationalization but rather about identifying genuine continuities that external observers, lacking access to internal experience, cannot perceive. The person who left law practice to become a craftsperson appears to have made a radical break. Still, suppose they can articulate that both vocations expressed commitment to precision and excellence, merely redirected from legal brief construction to furniture building. In that case, they experience continuity that validates their journey as coherent development rather than haphazard wandering. Research by narrative psychologist Michele Crossley examining individuals experiencing life transitions found that those who could construct such coherent accounts demonstrated significantly better psychological adjustment and higher satisfaction scores than those who experienced their histories as discontinuous sequences of unrelated episodes. The implication is profound: fulfillment may depend less on the objective trajectory one's life follows and more on one's capacity to perceive that trajectory as expressing persistent commitments and values, suggesting that narrative skill itself constitutes a prerequisite for fulfillment.

Existential Permission and the Authority to Satisfy

Perhaps the deepest requirement for personal fulfillment involves what we might call "existential permission", the capacity to authorize one's own life as sufficient without requiring external validation. This represents the culmination of psychological development, as described by the theorist Robert Kegan, a shift to a "self-transforming mind", a stage in which one's self-concept no longer depends on meeting standards established by others but rather on embodying principles one has consciously examined and endorsed. Kegan's research suggests that fewer than 20% of adults reach this developmental stage, with most remaining at earlier phases in which self-worth depends on either conforming to social expectations or differentiating oneself through rebellion against them, both positions ultimately granting external standards the authority to define adequacy. The person who seeks fulfillment while remaining at these earlier stages confronts an impossible task: their evaluative framework grants others the power to determine whether their life is sufficient, meaning satisfaction requires consensus that proves perpetually elusive. The colleague who questions their career choice, the parent who implies disappointment, the social media feed displaying others' achievements, all possess authority to generate feelings of inadequacy because the person hasn't yet claimed authority to declare their own life adequate, regardless of how it measures against alternative possibilities.

Existential permission doesn't involve arrogant dismissal of others' perspectives or narcissistic inflation of one's importance. Instead, it represents what philosopher Jean-Paul Sartre termed "radical freedom", recognition that one is ultimately responsible for the meaning one attributes to one's circumstances and choices. Sartre's claim that "existence precedes essence" means that humans aren't born with predetermined purposes they either fulfill or fail to achieve; instead, they create their purposes through how they live and what they commit to. This philosophical position has profound psychological implications: it means that no external authority can legitimately declare a life wasted or insufficient, because lives lack objective purposes against which they can be measured. The person who recognizes this achieves a particular kind of liberation; they become the legitimate judge of whether their life is proceeding adequately. This doesn't eliminate genuine failure or prevent legitimate criticism. Still, it does avoid the perpetual inadequacy that results from implicitly granting society, family, or peer groups the authority to define what one's life should accomplish. Research by psychologist Margie Lachman at Brandeis University examining "sense of control" across lifespan development found that individuals who maintained an internal locus of evaluation, believing that they, rather than external factors or other people, determined whether their lives were satisfactory, demonstrated remarkable resilience in the face of objective setbacks. Job loss, divorce, and health crises that devastated individuals with an external locus of evaluation produced manageable distress for those who had claimed existential permission to define their own success criteria.

The practical challenge involves how one acquires existential permission in cultures that systematically withhold it. Educational systems, employment structures, and social institutions typically reward compliance with pre-established standards rather than cultivating capacity for self-authorization. Students learn to satisfy teachers' requirements rather than develop autonomous judgment; employees learn to meet managers' expectations rather than define meaningful contribution; citizens learn to fulfill social roles rather than examine which roles deserve fulfillment. Breaking free from these conditioning patterns requires what psychologist Shoshana Zuboff calls "epistemic responsibility", the willingness to explore the origins of one's beliefs and standards rather than accepting them as given. The person who discovers that their career dissatisfaction stems from pursuing their parents' ambitions rather than their own, who recognizes that their consumption patterns reflect advertising manipulation rather than authentic desire, who realizes that their relationship expectations derive from cultural scripts rather than personal values, has begun the work of claiming existential permission. This examination often produces discomfort because it reveals how much of what one thought was freely chosen actually resulted from unconscious internalization of external standards. Yet this discomfort represents progress: recognizing that one's current life architecture reflects imported standards creates space to ask whether those standards deserve continued authority, and if not, what principles might replace them. The journey to fulfillment necessarily traverses this uncomfortable territory of discovering that much of what one thought constituted personal identity actually represents unexamined adoption of others' expectations, a discovery that, while destabilizing, opens the possibility of constructing identity on more conscious foundations.

The achievement of existential permission manifests in a particular quality of presence that others often recognize, even if they cannot name. The fulfilled person exhibits what Buddhists call "groundedness", a quality of being settled within themselves that doesn't depend on circumstances confirming their worth. They can acknowledge mistakes without experiencing existential threat, accept criticism without defensive reaction, and face uncertainty without panic, because their fundamental sense of life's adequacy doesn't require external validation or circumstantial stability. This groundedness differs markedly from the fragile confidence of someone whose self-assurance depends on continued success or social approval. Research by psychologist Kristin Neff examining self-compassion, the capacity to treat oneself with kindness during failure or difficulty, found that individuals high in self-compassion demonstrated greater psychological resilience, higher satisfaction, and better performance across domains compared to those high in self-esteem. The distinction matters: self-esteem depends on positive evaluation (I am good because I meet standards), while self-compassion involves basic acceptance (I am human and therefore inherently worthy of kindness regardless of performance). The person who has claimed existential permission operates from a self-compassion framework; they can acknowledge insufficiency in specific areas without experiencing those limitations as invalidating their existence. This creates the psychological safety necessary for genuine development, since one can only improve in domains where one feels secure enough to admit current inadequacy. The paradox is that personal fulfillment, often imagined as requiring achievement or self-optimization, actually becomes possible only when one has claimed permission to be inadequate, imperfect, and limited, because only then can one stop defending against the recognition of limitation and begin engaging honestly with one's actual, sufficient self.

===

About The Author

Nathaniel T. Brooks is a seasoned life coach, writer, and wellness advocate whose work explores the quiet power of living with intention. With over a decade of experience in personal development and transformative practice, Brooks has guided countless individuals toward clarity, resilience, and authentic fulfillment. His journey into behavioral science began with formal studies in Psychology and Behavioral Science. Still, it deepened through years of mentoring people who had achieved everything they were told to want, only to realize they still felt empty.

Blending evidence-based research with a grounded, humanistic philosophy, Brooks has built a reputation for cutting through the noise of the self-help industry with rare honesty. His voice is calm yet uncompromising, urging readers to let go of the constant chase for "more" and rediscover what it means to have enough. Through workshops, essays, and community work, he challenges the modern narrative of success, showing that contentment isn't complacency; it's courage.

The Book On Enough captures the essence of Brooks's philosophy: that fulfillment begins not with acquisition, but with alignment. Drawing on insights from psychology, minimalism, and mindful living, he offers a roadmap for those ready to recalibrate their relationship with ambition, possessions, and peace of mind. Written with warmth and conviction, the book invites readers to slow down, breathe deeper, and redefine success on their own terms.

When he isn't writing or coaching, Brooks can be found hiking quiet trails, unplugging from the digital rush, or sharing conversations that remind people of life's overlooked richness, the beauty of simply being here, and the freedom of realizing that what you have can finally be enough.

About The Publisher

Welcome to The Book On Publishing

At The Book On Publishing, we believe in rewriting the rules of learning. Whether you're chasing your next big idea, building a better life, or simply curious about what should have been taught in school, you've come to the right place.

We're a platform built for dreamers, doers, and lifelong learners, offering bold, practical books and tools that empower you to take charge of your journey. From real-world skills to mindset mastery, we publish the book on what matters.

No fluff. No lectures. Just what you need to know, delivered with clarity, purpose, and a spark of curiosity.

Start exploring. Start growing. Start writing your story.

Read more at https://thebookon.ca.

Acknowledgment of AI Assistance

Portions of this book were developed with the support of AI. While every word has been carefully reviewed and refined by the author, AI served as a valuable tool for brainstorming, editing, and structuring ideas. Its assistance helped accelerate the creative process and bring clarity to complex topics.

www.ingramcontent.com/pod-product-compliance
Lightning Source LLC
Chambersburg PA
CBHW071732120626
46550CB00002B/493